Somebody Turned on a Tap in These Kids

Somebody Turned on a Tap in These Kids

POETRY AND YOUNG PEOPLE TODAY

Edited by NANCY LARRICK

 A DELTA BOOK

A DELTA BOOK
Published by Dell Publishing Co., Inc.
750 Third Avenue
New York, N.Y. 10017

ACKNOWLEDGMENTS

Grateful acknowledgment is made for permission to use excerpts from the following copyrighted material:

What the Heart Knows Today

From *The Crock of Gold* by James Stephens. Copyright 1912 by The Macmillan Company. Reprinted by permission of Mrs. Iris Wise, The Macmillan Company of New York, Macmillan & Co. Ltd., London; and The Macmillan Company of Canada Ltd.

From *A Tune Beyond Us* by Myra Cohn Livingston, ed. Harcourt Brace Jovanovich, Inc., 1960.

"Michael From Mountains," words and music by Joni Mitchell. Copyright © 1968. Reprinted by permission of the publisher, Siquomb Publishing Corp.

From "Richard Cory." Copyright © 1966 by Charing Cross Music, Inc. Used with permission of the Publisher.

"Getting Better," lyrics from *The Beatles Illustrated Lyrics* edited by Alan Aldridge. Lyrics copyright © 1962, 1963, 1964, 1965, 1966, 1967, 1968, 1969 by Northern Songs Limited (London). Illustrations and text copyright © 1969 by Alan Aldridge Associates Limited (London). A Seymour Lawrence Book, Delacorte Press/New York.

From "At The Zoo." Copyright © 1967 by Paul Simon. Used with permission of the publisher, Charing Cross Music, Inc.

From *Bestiary/Bestiario* by Pablo Neruda, English translation copy-

"I Will Never, Never in My Long Life" by Deborah Crawford. Copyright © 1970 by The Voice of the Children, Inc. From *Expand*. Volume 1, number 2.

"April 4, 1968" by Michael Goode. Copyright © 1968 by *The Village Voice, Inc.*

"My Life" by Juanita Bryant, "The Jazz World" by Michael Gill, "Talking" by Michael Goode, "I've Seen Enough" by Christopher Meyer, and "The Air Is Dirty" by Glen Thompson. Copyright © 1968 by The Voice of the Children, Inc. "Addition Problem" by Michael Goode and "The Grey Sky" by Linda X. Copyright © 1969 by The Voice of the Children, Inc. From *The Voice of the Children*. Reprinted by permission of Holt, Rinehart & Winston, Inc.

"Darkling Afternoon" by Anthony Holmes, "Dew" and "The Roaring Wind" by Carlton Minor. Copyright © 1968 by The Voice of the Children, Inc. "My Joy Is a Thing of the Past," "When You Burn You Earn," and "While I Wait Myself Becomes My Future Fate" by Linda X. Copyright © 1969 by The Voice of the Children, Inc.

It's Not a Joyous City

"We Real Cool" from *Selected Poems* by Gwendolyn Brooks. Copyright © 1959 by Gwendolyn Brooks. Reprinted by permission of Harper & Row, Publishers, Inc.

"City" from *Golden Slippers: An Anthology of Negro Poetry,* by Arna Bontemps, ed. (Harper & Row, Publishers, Inc.). Copyright © 1941 by Langston Hughes. Reprinted by permission of Harold Ober Associates Incorporated.

"Is God Dead?" by Martin Radcliffe. Reprinted by permission of his agent, Mrs. Isabel K. Heller.

"Taught Me Purple" by Evelyn Tooley Hunt as published in *Negro Digest* (February 1964). Reprinted by permission of *Negro Digest* and Evelyn Tooley Hunt.

Experiment in the Inner City

"The Language." Copyright © 1964 Robert Greeley, is reprinted by permission by Charles Scribner's Sons from *Words* by Robert Creeley.

"I," Says the Poem

Contents

Poetry That's Real   NANCY LARRICK   I

"What the Heart Knows Today"   MYRA COHN LIVINGSTON   6

The Poetic Language of Childhood   CLAUDIA LEWIS   27

"Talk to Mice and Fireplugs . . ."   KARLA KUSKIN   38

Poetry in the Classroom   NANCY LARRICK   49

Children and the Hungering For   JUNE JORDAN   56

It's Not a Joyous City   NANCY LARRICK   73

Straight Talk From Teenagers
WARREN DOTY, SAMUEL ROBINSON, AND STUDENTS   78

Experiment in the Inner City
FLORENCE HOWE AND BARBARA DANISH   106

A Dialogue of Poetry   RICHARD LEWIS   141

"I," Says the Poem   EVE MERRIAM   147

Notes   167
Index   171

SOMEBODY TURNED ON A TAP IN THESE KIDS grew out of the Poetry Festival sponsored by the School of Education of Lehigh University in the spring of 1969. More than 1,000 people participated—teachers, librarians, poets, critics, anthologists, inner-city teenagers and college students. Papers read during the festival and talks and discussion taped that day make up the greater part of the book.

The title is from a statement by Gerald Jackson about the "eruption of poetic activity" in the 1969 Yale Summer High School for Upward Bound Students, of which he was assistant director. "Somebody turned on a tap in these kids," he said, "and the poetry just kept coming."

—N.L.

Somebody Turned on a Tap in These Kids

NANCY LARRICK

Poetry That's Real

There is a hunger for poetry among young people today that leaves "The Village Blacksmith" generation incredulous. The young of all ages are reading and writing poetry because they love it. Boys and girls are even producing their own mimeographed magazines of poetry. Inner-city teenagers go to a Miss Ebonette beauty contest to applaud the reading of students' poems.

These things are happening all over the country. From a church basement in Bedford-Stuyvesant, Brooklyn, poets of from ten to fourteen are writing, reading and publishing every Saturday. In a consolidated rural school near Revere, Pennsylvania, fourth-graders produced their own *Prayers from the Ark,* inspired by poetry written originally in French for adults. From Berkeley and Watts, from Rabun Gap, Georgia, from inner-city Philadelphia, from Baltimore and Washington and Tucson comes a mounting stream of poetry by young writers.

Recently the *Yale Alumni Magazine* included four pages of poetry written by Upward Bound students enrolled in the Yale Summer High School. These poems, we are told, are only a tiny fraction of the summer's output.

In the 1969 Poetry Search conducted by the Creativity

Research Institute of Fordham University, fourth-, fifth- and sixth-graders of the New York metropolitan area submitted over 21,000 of their poems. *The Poetry Search Anthology,* which grew out of the Fordham project, is made up of 131 poems of these children—some of them rollicking, frolicking; some of them daydreaming, reflecting, caring. Minor notes of loneliness and anxiety pierce many of their songs.

In almost every city we are finding locally published collections of poetry by children and young adults.

Publishers' lists show an extraordinary upsurge in the number of poetry books in print. Youngsters are helping to create the demand. Not only do they read widely from books available on library shelves, but they go out and buy. Those over ten are turning more and more to adult poetry by such writers as William Carlos Williams, Gregory Corso, Lawrence Ferlinghetti and Kenneth Patchen. LeRoi Jones, rarely on school library lists, is a favorite among city teenagers, who buy their own paperback editions.

But printed poetry is only part of the story. Poetry recorded for listening is a magnet to thousands of young people, who particularly like to hear a poet reading his own work. Lacking the recorded voices of many of their favorite poets, young people tape their own reading of these poets, sometimes dubbing in background music which, for them, adds to the mood of the poems.

The person over twenty-five can hardly grasp the significance of recordings in the lives of those younger than he. Record-industry spokesmen say that 85 percent of all single records are bought by people under twenty-five. When they are not playing their own records, they are listening to recorded music on radio. The transistor radio goes along with the teenager as surely as a wristwatch goes with the adult.

The music they hear is often close to poetry, for these

young listeners prefer folksongs above all else. Sometimes they are old songs revived by new voices, such as "Turn, Turn, Turn," sung by Judy Collins. Or they may be as critically contemporary as "Alice's Restaurant" by Arlo Guthrie. Whether old or new, they have the rhythm, the imagination and usually the emotional pull which are the earmarks of poetry. To listen to the modern song of protest is to get involved, and involvement is just what modern children expect.

Television has taught them that. Marshall McLuhan explains that some three million dots stream across the TV screen per second, always moving, never making one fixed picture. The viewer becomes the picture maker, the participant, who selects the dots from which he creates the image—a process completely different from photo and movie viewing. "The movie viewer remains detached and is engaged in looking *at* the screen," he explains. "The TV viewer *is* the screen." This sense of involvement is what enthralls children, according to Dr. McLuhan.

Poetry, beyond any other literary form, solicits participation from the listener or reader. Indeed, some people insist that a poem is not complete until there is a partner adding his own experiences and feelings to those of the poet.

Passion for music and poetry is one of the distinguishing features of an oral-language culture. Before Gutenberg froze language into print, people heard more language than they read. Wandering minstrels and storytellers brought literature to crowds in the village square or courtyard. Those who came to listen were soon singing or chanting repeated lines and sometimes adding new stanzas on the old pattern.

Now in the age of radio, television and recordings, oral language reigns again, more insistently than before. Children hear language every waking hour and often in their sleeping hours as well. They are entranced by the electronic voices of the Beatles, Simon and Garfunkel, Joni Mitchell and all the rest. Without once seeing the words in print, they absorb every line of such songs as "The Harper Valley P.T.A." and "Alice's Restaurant."

During the past few years I have been trying to learn more about children's response to poetry in this oral-language culture of ours. Through a Lehigh University workshop for elementary-school teachers, now in its sixth year, more than a hundred teachers, with the help of their pupils, have tried to find the most effective ways of getting children involved in poetry. I think a first-grader from a low-income housing project summarized our findings when he said to his teacher one day, "When can we *do* poetry?" At first, I was repelled by the idea of *doing* poetry, but when I visited that class, I saw what this boy meant. Every child was involved in poetry through the firsthand experiences which their teacher made part of the class day.

Many of these youngsters were singing and chanting the jump-rope jingles and counting-out rhymes they had learned on the playground or sidewalk. Others were reciting favorite poems in unison, sometimes with a solo voice or with alternating parts, sometimes adding new lines to fit the old pattern. Others were swinging into impromptu dramatization as the words were read or sung by their classmates. The same kind of involvement appeals tremendously to older children as well, once they feel free to choose the poems they like and then to present them in their way.

The poems they choose are strikingly different from those once considered the poetic fare of childhood. Modern children just don't warm up to the "modest violet" and "sweet-scented hay." Instead, they go for poems that are "real," as they put it.

The search for what is real has led many a poet and his readers to topics once thought of as unpoetic: traffic lights, for example, and escalators, subways and littered sidewalks. On crowded streets and in cluttered hallways man's inhumanity to man shows up dramatically. Adults who have equated poetry with "a host of golden daffodils" may find it difficult to accept this harsh reality for children. Yet this is the children's world, too. Even suburban and rural youngsters have been brought into urban deprivation and protest via television. And in every home the televised horrors of war are shown in brutal detail.

It should not surprise us, then, to find that today's children seek the realistic poetry of bolder voices, speaking in a blunt conversational style. They like poems which debunk the phony and unveil hypocrisy. I think this is one of the reasons why they are held by Eve Merriam's *The Inner City Mother Goose,* which is a biting commentary on the injustices of the American ghetto.

"This is real," explained one fourteen-year-old. "The trouble with poetry at school is it's all covered over with the beautiful."

The poetry young people want today is real. It relates to the world they know, and it invites them to become physically and emotionally involved. Involvement is what they demand.

MYRA COHN LIVINGSTON

MYRA COHN LIVINGSTON, author of 13 books of poetry for children, and editor of several poetry anthologies, has written numerous articles about poetry for children.

"What the Heart Knows Today"

All of us blithely admit to the dizzying pace of change in this crazy, exciting world of ours. Nothing seems immune to it—not our institutions of learning; not our morals or ethics; not even poetry.

But there are those who cling to poetry with a capital P as though it alone were sacred and impervious to change. They seek a definition which will be established forever as the *sine qua non,* and they search with fervor for poems which will hold up immortal truths, untouchable beauties as shining precepts for young minds. In quoting Keats, "Poetry . . . should strike the reader as a wording of his own highest thoughts," they interpret "highest" as a synonym for lofty, ethereal, moral, refined contemplations and meditations. In this guise poetry becomes a spokesman for ideas and ideals reserved for special occasions, a Sunday sort of quasi-religious fervor meant not only to uplift but also to drive out the baser emotions. This is often labeled "Truth," and it is shrouded by such fuzzy phrases as "the wisdom of a poem," "the highlighting of a truth," "beauty of expression." This would almost imply that poetry is another language, one in which the average human has no discourse, or at best only during moments of high spiritual elevation.

In the March 1968 issue of *Elementary English,* a teacher expresses tremendous enthusiasm for poetry and particularly the writing of poetry by children. She is quick to acknowledge that poetry is made up of all elements of life; yet, what follows demands our closer scrutiny. "Any theme which the teacher feels will lend itself to poetic expression can be used," she writes—"aspects of life important to children like holidays, fire, people, water, the fair" and so forth. "The teacher must be alive to the possibilities inherent in situations and judge for herself whether or not certain themes are apt for poetry-writing. She must recognize that in some instances a poetic interpretation would be unsuitable."[1]

This teacher, in other words, is paying lip service to the idea that everything in man's experience is subject for a poem, but she is in actuality denying the children the right to put this idea into practice. She will remain the arbiter of what is fit for poetic expression and what is not. People, holidays, fire—fine!—but stay away from any theme or subject of which the teacher does not approve. One's mind is tempted to wander: How will she quash what a child may actually be thinking of—war perhaps, gangsters, fights, prejudice, his dislikes, his hatreds? Automatically, therefore, poetry becomes a capital-P subject, one reserved only for teacher-approved feelings and observations confined (in her own words) to "the finest ingredients of language."

Pablo Neruda in his essay "Towards an Impure Poetry" tells of the beauty that is in the worn, dusty wheel, the footprint and fingerprint, the used objects of life. Theodore Roethke asks for a reader with respect and curiosity toward poetry, the sort of curiosity which will make a man unafraid to look at a world different from his own, which will allow him to perceive the true emotions of another, and not to hide in fear from emotion. And these feelings are echoed by a myriad of other poets who recognize that poetry contains all the emotions of man; not alone those of joy, but those which are questioning, tragic or unsure; not only the pure, but the impure; not alone the engaging of the mind, but the music and rhythms of the body. If, therefore, one is willing to accept such a poetry, one must view with alarm the teacher who will decide in both the reading and the writing of poetry what is "suitable" or "unsuitable" for the creative expression of children.

Discussing the writing of inner-city children, Nancy Larrick tells of students who were unwilling to show their poems to teachers.[2] Usually, she discovered, the reason was the same: "No use. Wouldn't like it." It is as if the children inherently know that many of the emotions which they feel and translate into writing will not meet the standardization of what the teacher will accept or attempt to understand. Nor will their lack of so-called poetic language suffice for the capital-P poetry.

But the situation is changing. The social and economic pressures of our age have forced us, sometimes happily in peace, sometimes unhappily in violence, to recognize that Puritanical strictures on human emotions *must* go. Some of the recently published writing of ghetto children attests to the fact that there are teachers who remain receptive to the true emotions and feelings of children and who will permit these children to express themselves in whatever form of language they can. Oftentimes this writing takes the form of what I term "hate poems." If in a privileged, leisurely and highly advantaged school the hates reflect jealousy of a girl who snares all the boys, the burning smog or the cafeteria hamburgers, why can they not, in disadvantaged areas, direct themselves to leaky plumbing, gang fights, and racial and religious unrest?

Michael Sanchez, sixteen years old, comments on this in his poem "Yes . . . We Learned":

They taught us to hate
   like machines to be programmed.
They taught us to hate
   those communist monsters.

They taught us to serve
   like ants serve their queen.
They taught us to serve
   that whitewashed american
   power structure.

We learn to hate
   that society that bred us
We learn to hate
   the ignorance they left us in.

We learn to serve
   only our instincts, our passions
We learn to serve
   only ourselves.[3]

Another Los Angeles teenager, Olga Ceballos, says it like this:

   I refuse to identify myself
   with any country or race.
   If I say I am from a certain
   place on this earth,
   people will expect me to
   glorify it, and swear to die
   for it. I wish to glorify
   the whole earth, and die
   only for the existence
   of all life on earth. If
   I tell that I am of a

certain race of humans,
people will again expect me
to glorify these people and
die for their existence only.
I wish to glorify the
entire human race and
die for the existence of
all men.[4]

Yet hate or protest poems are but one small facet of the range of emotions for which we search in our children's expression. Another small group is the poems which come to us as perfect published examples of the child's art, usually extolling the beauties of nature. In between there is the huge bulk of so-called creative writing, never seen beyond the classroom or the home, sometimes bound into a sheaf of writing that goes on display at Open House or Book Fair time. It is this writing with which I am concerned because, for the most part, it reflects most aptly the crying need for a new approach to creative writing in our classrooms across the country.

We will not see, I believe, truly creative writing until we recognize that real feelings, real emotions give rise to a force within the individual that creates the form and words of poetry. It is *not* the form and the words that create the force. It is not the simile, the metaphor, the adjective, the strong verb, the alliteration, the rhyme or nonrhyme we must focus attention on—these are but the tools of poetry. It is not the 17-syllable haiku, the limerick, the quatrain, the couplet, the sonnet—these are but the forms of poetry. It is not these we must praise as expressions of a student's creative ability but rather the force of his feelings, his emotions, in whatever form or language they happen to come out.

No one, I feel, has said it so well as did Randall Jarrell in

The Bat-Poet.[5] The bat, having written a poem about an owl who nearly killed him, reads his poem to the mockingbird, whose songs he greatly admires. And while the mockingbird finds the bat's poem technically accomplished, he fails utterly to realize, as does a little chipmunk, that more important than iambic pentameter or the rhyme scheme is the poem's ability to scare, to convey that death swoop of the owl which so frightened the bat that the emotion became force enough for a poem.

It is this ability within the poem to "scare," this emotion of fear spilling over to the language and the form and all becoming one, which is at the crux of what we seek in children's creative writing. Not the change of rhyme scheme, not the iambic trimeter ("I just made it like holding your breath," the bat tells the mockingbird), not the technicalities, but rather the force of the fear conveyed through the telling.

There is, to my way of thinking, too much satisfaction by parents, educators and the children themselves in accepting the form rather than the force. Patrick Groff speaks of a "doggerel called creative writing" which invades classrooms and schoolrooms.[6] I have seen much of it, and so have you. Happily, we are no longer so concerned with those who copy patterns or fill in blanks; the beginning acceptance of blank verse, free verse, haiku has helped somewhat to break the rhyme barrier, but we have a long way to go before we can succeed in recognizing that the tools of poetry are not poetry. We all seem to accept the fact that poetry is metaphorical writing, of course, but the endless exercises in creating metaphor and simile practiced by so many well-meaning teachers have really nothing to do with the force of individual expression behind the poem itself. It is all very well for a child to say that a two-inch-diameter concrete pipe is like a straw for a giant, or that a tree is an old bearded man; it is fine to rhyme "borrow" with "sorrow" or "tomorrow"; it is splendid to say that clouds are "airy, fairy pillows" or that the "cantankerous cat crept cautiously"— but what then? It may help develop the imagination, it may be useful for language arts, literature and English study, but it is not the stuff of which "heightened consciousness" is most powerfully created.

Please let me make it clear that I am not opposed to teaching or to learning about figures of speech, about the tools of poetry; nor am I opposed to form in poetry. Far from it. But I feel, from some years of experience, from many a misstep in poetry sharing and creative writing, that these are secondary to the tremendous force of self-expression which springs from genuine and real emotions. No teacher has it within his power to teach another human being to write; all that the teacher can do is to awaken response, to help develop sensitivities and make a child aware of his identity and individuality and, if he is lucky, to help that child find a form in which he can best express himself.

In my own classes in creative writing, I strive for one thing above all: that whatever is written is honestly felt and put down as such, no matter what the form or language. This inevitably means that the only thing which creative writing and English have in common is the words of the English language. For me creative writing means a time for honest expression with illegible scribbling, if need be, incorrect spelling, poor punctuation, grammatical error and oftentimes a butchering of the king's English.

I have always asked two things of my classes which remain our guideposts: (1) Tell me something I have never heard before, or (2) tell me something I already know in a new way, *your* way. At the basis of these principles lies doom for the cliché, the overworked adjective, the tired metaphor and simile, the meaningless rhyme. And the serendipity of it all is that seldom, as a teacher, do I have to catch these things myself; the children see and do it among and for themselves.

Jared, who after a year has made the plunge to free himself from hackneyed rhyme, beams as he reads his cat poem:

> He purrs.
> I see him.
> He dashes behind a tree.
> He leaves like a bolt of lightning.
> He's gone.

Steve raises his hand. "That's a cliché, 'a bolt of lightning.' " And Jared sighs and resolves to give it another try.

Anna, who clings to rhyme and still feels poetry cannot be without it, reads her cat poem:

> Shimmering, reflected in the lake
> Selene, goddess of the moon's namesake
> Fluid her movement so unreal
> Craving, lacking a good meal. . . .

The poem read, hands shoot up everywhere: "lacking a good meal" in juxtaposition with a goddess? Never. At the last revision the line went "Before her, all beings kneel."

Mark reads his poem about a cat:

> Individual feet jump
> like a pad of dough
> Poke out 2 eyes
> and it will smother
> you, make sick
> noises, fall
> into your corner and
> break atmosphere
> or climb into mind
> and scratch

I want to pull off
and throw at ground
but   dead
come alive in mind
and stings.

"I don't know," says Steven, shaking his head. "Your poems always sound good and they've got good words in them, but I don't understand them."

And then Steve reads his:

The cat stares, very intent,
I have disturbed her,
She is no longer content.

Curious me, I walk toward
Her only domain.
Tense now, she leaves her small board

And now with silent motion
She jumps to her kits
And shows all her devotion.

"I don't like it," he is quick to add, "I don't like the last line. It's awful. 'Devotion' isn't right."

I must presume Steve hasn't found the right word yet.

My text is from James Stephens' *The Crock of Gold*. The philosopher has been to see Angus Og. "I have learned," said the philosopher, "that the head does not listen until the heart has heard, and what the heart knows today the head will understand tomorrow."[7]

What do our hearts know today, we who are teachers and

parents a generation removed from our children? I suspect that, when all is said and done, human emotions have not, for the most part, changed so very much. It is simply in our approach to them that things have changed, in the forms and rhythms in which they express themselves. I think, most optimistically, that we have grown out of that period when we regard some particular and certain poem as the be-all and end-all of literature and that we are willing to try new poems, new forms of expression, that we are facing the fact that each child we meet is an individual and may not fit into a mold whereby he must automatically learn to love and recite "Invictus" or "The Village Blacksmith," but instead choose something which appeals to him.

As teachers, I believe we have a tremendous task in the area of sharing poetry with children, poetry that is relevant to our age, poetry that speaks to our children. It is time, I believe, that we throw out an entire body of poetry that is no longer meaningful to children, either because of its archaic diction or because it, like its age, concentrated on a point of view, an experience which does not relate to our times. There are still in the classrooms of today many of the same old saws, dragged out decade after decade, which not only fail to engage our children's hearts but build up a horror of capital-P poetry; poems of sentimentality for bygone eras, poems of didactic exhortations, poems which extol a world our children will never know and to which they cannot relate, poems of experiences a child has never felt. There are many who believe that poetry is not the realm of children, that because of its great themes of love and death, it should be reserved for later years. I do not think this is the point; I feel that certain kinds of love are part of children; certain kinds of death can be, too. I believe a wide range of emotions should be presented, but such poems should be chosen wisely and in the metaphorical guise which will appeal to children because of necessarily limited experience as well as with an ear and eye to the language and rhythms of our day. It was with this belief that I compiled the anthology of poetry entitled *A Tune Beyond Us*.[8]

There *are* new forms, new rhythms, new language at work, yet I cannot begin to explain to you my own sense of puzzlement when I recently undertook a bit of research in the field of pop music. I was somewhat prepared for the beat of rock but amazingly unprepared for the lyrics. For hours and hours I have listened to the Beatles, Joan Baez, Judy Collins, Jimi Hendrix, the Cream, the Doors, Three Dog Night. These are the words, the sounds to which children listen today: the Rod McKuens, the Leonard Cohens, the John Lennons, the Simon and Garfunkels. And the fact is that the young people are listening to these singers with their hearts—and their hearts tell them that there is something to hear. I do not speak now of folk music or the love songs with which any adolescent's heart (or grown-up's, for that matter) is bound to swell. But I do know that the Beatles are a cult who weave a power unsurpassed by even Shakespeare.

Now I can hear and I can listen, and I can unabashedly say that the musical invention (for I have been a professional musician myself) in the Beatles is astounding. "It's *not* noise," many young people have told me. "It's sounds." New sounds, inventive sounds, sounds that are better heard through special equipment, no doubt. It's a new beat, too, and in most instances difficult to capture by the lyricism. But the words—some of them puzzled and disturbed me for weeks. I could find symbolism; I could find metaphor and simile and rhyme in a Joni Mitchell song, "Michael from Mountains":

> Michael wakes you up with sweets,
> he takes you up streets
> and the rain comes down;

Sidewalk markets locked up tight
and umbrellas bright
on a grey background;
There's oil on the puddles
in taffeta patterns
that run down the drain,
In colored arrangements that Michael will change with
a stick that he found.

Michael from Mountains,
Go where you will go to,
Know that I will know you,
Someday I may know you very well.[9]

I could find sentiment and simple beauty in Simon and Gar-
funkel's "Old friends, old friends/ Sit on their parkbench like
bookends."[10] I could find protest in dozens of songs, including
some as innocuous as the takeoff on "Richard Cory":

But I work in his factory
And I curse the life I'm living
And I curse my poverty
And I wish that I could be
And I wish that I could be
And I wish that I could be
Richard Cory.[11]

Some mild protest against the Establishment in the Beatles'
"Getting Better":

I used to get mad at school
The teachers that taught me weren't cool.
You're holding me down, turning me round,
Filling me up with your rules.[12]

Protests against parents, institutions, war, policemen and hypocrisy; cries for friends, for love, for sunshine, for uncorrupted nature; these are not difficult to plumb, and if I am still puzzling over "Lucy in the Sky with Diamonds" or "A Day in the Life" (both by the Beatles) or "Priests" by Leonard Cohen, I am assured by my young friends that I don't get the point at all. "No meaning," they tell me, "just feel. You can read anything in it you want to or no meaning at all."

But the Beatles, above all, interested and intrigued me. "You just don't understand," a twenty-year-old friend told me. "The beauty of the Beatles is not only their sound and invention and poking fun, but what they say is *true!* It's never been said before that way. Every time something happens to me, I think of a word or a phrase in a Beatle song. It's there. It's just true."

I answered him at the time: It's in Shakespeare, too; it's in Coleridge and Chaucer or Jiménez or Pushkin, García Lorca, William Butler Yeats. Where were you? You attended the finest public and private schools, an outstanding prep school for boys; now you attend a first-rate university. Why didn't you find it there?

The last question was rhetorical, for I think I know too well why you didn't find it, and why your peers or their younger sisters and brothers aren't finding it. It was because in most classrooms there was so much attention to facts, to hunting out figures of speech, to classifying literature, so much attention to words in dictionaries and the birth date of the poet that the force was neglected. So much stuffing of literature into the test tube that what the poet had to say of the human condition, of emotions and feelings, was of little importance. Unless it fitted into a test question, unless it was a fact with which to astound a school board, it was of no use.

But you are a human being, your heart cried for more, and

you think the Beatles invented it. You believe now that an older generation cannot understand; you must escape from them. You are willing to accept the Beatles' language, their words to express what man has always expressed. You find in a "yellow submarine," "tangerine trees," "marshmallow fields" the escape; you find in the symbolism of the pop song—the sun, the rain, the park, the sea—something which speaks to your heart. All right, young man, so be it. If their music, their mode speak to you in the rhythms and forms and sounds of your day, as the songs of my day sometimes spoke to me, praise be.

I do share with you, I do understand the enthusiasm that in the Beatles, at least, there is a force which dictates the form and the words, and not the other way around.

But there is a footnote: because although I can understand all of this, the emotional feelings and forces which give rise to protest, to poking fun, to seeking out friends, to fantasy and the beauties of nature in a sometimes trying world, still I must counter with one last thought. There is only one thing that bothers me and that is the drugs. Drugs are the key to what often appears in your songs as "heightened consciousness," the symbolism of Mr. K. and Mr. H., the girl with the kaleidoscope eyes, flying, turning you on. You were never allowed to know that one can see color, be turned on, become sensitive and aware without drugs. You were cheated, young man, of the expression of your real emotions.

Perhaps, perhaps, if there had been a few teachers along the way who had ferreted out those poems, those works of literature to astound and amaze you and stack up against the Beatles and their imitators; perhaps if, one day, you had been allowed to express the joy which you felt (undrugged) and create something of your own, you would understand my generation better.

Early this month I took to my class a recording of a Simon and Garfunkel song, "At the Zoo." It goes like this:

> Someone told me
> It's all happening at the zoo.
> I do believe it,
> I do believe it's true.
>
> It's a light and tumble journey
> From the East Side to the park,
> Just a fine and fancy ramble
> To the zoo.
> But you can take the crosstown bus
> if it's raining or it's cold.
> And the animals will love it
> If you do.
>
> Somethin' tells me
> It's all happening at the zoo.
> I do believe it.
> I do believe it's true.
>
> The monkeys stand for honesty,
> Giraffes are insincere,
> And the elephants are kindly but
> They're dumb.
> Orangutans are skeptical
> Of changes in their cages,
> And the zookeeper is very fond of rum.
> Zebras are reactionaries,
> Pigeons plot in secrecy,
> And hamsters turn on frequently.
> What a gas! You gotta come and see
> At the zoo.[13]

Following this, I read from Walt Whitman's *Leaves of Grass:*

I think I could turn and live with animals, they are so
placid and self contain'd,
I stand and look at them long and long.

They do not sweat and whine about their condition,
They do not lie awake in the dark and weep for their
sins,
They do not make me sick discussing their duty to God,
Not one is dissatisfied, not one is demented with the
mania of owning things,
Not one kneels to another, nor to his kind that lived
thousands of years ago,
Not one is respectable or unhappy over the whole earth.
So they show their relations to me and I accept them,
They bring me tokens of myself, they evince them plainly
in their possession.

And then I read some of Pablo Neruda's "Bestiary":

If I could speak with birds,
with oysters and with little lizards,
with the foxes of the Dark Forest,
with the exemplary penguins;
if the sheep,
the languid woolly lap dogs,
the cart horses would understand me;
if I could discuss things with cats,
if hens would listen to me!

It has never occurred to me to speak
with elegant animals

he continues, but rather to talk to flies, dogs, rabbits, rumi-
nants, pigs, frogs.

> Fleas interest me so much
> that I let them bite me for hours.
> They are perfect, ancient, Sanskrit,
> machines that admit of no appeal.
> They do not bite to eat,
> they bite only to jump;
> they are the dancers of the celestial sphere,
> delicate acrobats
> in the softest and most profound circus;
> let them gallop on my skin,
> divulge their emotions,
> amuse themselves with my blood,
> but someone should introduce them to me.
> I want to know them closely.
> I want to know what to rely on.

Neruda ends his poem this way:

> I want to speak with many things
> and I will not leave this planet
> without knowing what I came to seek,
> without investigating this matter,
> and people do not suffice for me,
> I have to go much further
> and I have to go much closer.

> Therefore, gentlemen, I am going
> to converse with a horse.
> May the poetess excuse me,

and the professor forgive me.
My whole week is taken up,
I have to listen to a confusion of talk.

What was the name of that cat?

"How do you look at animals?" I asked my class. "Did
Simon and Garfunkel, did Whitman, did Neruda speak for
you?" It was an experiment. I had to find out how far I was
going off the road.

And last week the last of the animal poems came in, and al-
though there was some adverse comment on the choice of ad-
jectives, which will be amended in time, I give it to you now.
It is titled "Zoo":

> The lion bristles in his cage
> As you go by with peanuts
> For the elephants
> The elephants
> The elephants
>
> The hippos lounge in murky depths
> As you go by with smelly fish
> For the polar bears
> The polar bears
> The polar bears
>
> The parrots scream in stinky cages
> As you go by with carrots
> For the zebras
> The zebras
> The zebras

The ghettos cry with all their dirt
As we go by with food and money
For other countries
Other countries
Other countries

What the heart knows today—what my heart knows today —is that we must ever be on the lookout for the child who will write with full emotions. I know it is dangerous ground. I have been there. It is not easy to ask a child to tell you in his writing what he is really thinking, to bare his soul. It is an act which must be treated with the utmost respect, for matters of the heart and emotions are demanding of respect. It is much easier, I know, to assign a safe and suitable, appropriate subject or theme, to be able to display at Open House pleasant rhymes, pleasant verse.

But let us make that extra effort which will yield individuals of self-identity, of real feelings, rather than those who write to gain teacher approval—that effort which lands us on our faces many times. For there are some children who can never and will never unbend. I remember vividly one boy who was an honors student, armed with facts and quick to recognize meanings. He tried, he really tried, but at the end of the year I felt I had failed completely to impart any of the joy that made up the creative act. I discussed him with another teacher. "Don't feel so badly," she told me. "One day I took him a flower, and what did he do? He counted the petals."

There will always be the petal counters, I guess, but there may be a few who may somehow be touched, however hopeless it seems. A friend of mine, a librarian at an experimental school, called me about a month ago. She had been teaching a creative-writing group for six weeks and felt she had made little progress. There were no "visible effects" from the hours and

hours she had put into her work. I know what she means, be-
cause the countless times I have shared poetry with children,
shared poetry or my thoughts on poetry or writing, very seldom
yield any tangible effects. But I think of Henry Adams, who in
his years at Harvard felt that if he could reach one boy in a
class of 400, it was well worth the effort. And I think of the
times someone may come up and say, "You remember that
poem you read about pigs two years ago? Where can I find it?"

I want to show you a poem written by Lloyd in the eighth
grade. Just now he is in the ninth, and the last ballad, for which
he composed music as well as lyrics, was about the awful cafe-
teria hamburgers. He happened to read it one day during class
when the director of the elementary schools, along with as-
sorted dignitaries, came to pay us a visit. Just now Lloyd's writ-
ing verges on protest—over war, over hippies, over slogans,
over the hypocrisies he finds about him. This one is titled "To
Algebra":

> I'm trying to analyze this flower
> By using the addition property of equality,
> By computating the bisymmetry,
> Or maybe the multiplication
> > Property of order.
> By adding the yellow on the border:
> > A + B = C if and only if there is a number q
> > such that flowers can be thought of
> > either in Algebraic or Numerical terms.
> The stem, I find, is 4.5253 inches
> > Long.
> And yet the check says I am wrong.
> This flower—it does not belong
> In this great and modern world.

It bends too much for my liking,
Better work out what's the matter,
Oh no—my problem almost done
Unnumerical rain begins to patter—
Computate the difference.
All in vain—
This is the breaking of my brain!

I have a gnawing notion that it is up to us to make this flower—this flower with which so many songs abound, this flower pasted like a brand on our young peoples' notebooks, their dresses and jackets and hearts—fit back into the world. We can do it by listening to the hearts of our children, by restoring to a whole the entire range of emotions in the poetry we share, in the writing we seek; not being content with ends but searching for means; not asking for visible, beneficial effects and immediate, perfectly formed poems, but rather ferreting out the force which gives life to a developing human being. Not asking that children comprehend—but that they apprehend.

"The universal need of the young," says Harold Taylor, "is for a mode of expression through which they can say to the world something of their own in a way which is their own."[15]

The Beatles have done it. We can, too.

CLAUDIA LEWIS

CLAUDIA LEWIS, Professor of Education at Bank
Street College of Education in New York, has
written several monographs about the language of
children, as well as four books for children, including
Poems of Earth and Space.

The Poetic Language of Childhood

When we speak of "the poetic language of childhood," prob-
ably most of us think first of all of the striking metaphors and
similes young children coin with such apparent ease. One of
my favorite examples is the comment of a three-year-old upon
seeing for the first time a bunch of blue grapes: "Oh, blueber-
ries on the cob!" We adults, caught in the grooves of our
clichés, delight in this fresh image, its element of surprise, and
the unexpected likeness it reveals to us. Poetic language, yes,
for poets tell us that it is the thrust toward metaphor that
makes for greatness in poetry.

But we do the child an injustice if we simply label him a
"natural poet" and forget that he is one because he is attempt-
ing to grapple with the world and understand and name what
he does not know by associating it with what he does know. He
is forming his concepts, organizing his knowledge. As he puts
two and two together, trying to see relationships that help him
grasp meanings, he does indeed emerge as a poetic—or creative
—thinker, unconfined by the hedges that have sprung up
around us who have stopped looking for new insights into the
ordinary. But this is just the child's natural growth process—

one that all of us could aid and abet in many ways, in the class-room.

And because the child is young, his thinking has what seems to us a daring, fresh quality. As he invents his metaphors and discovers the images he needs, he leaps ahead in his own way, unaware of the conventions of our adult thought. What he says carries the stamp of his own unique individuality. Who but a young child would know—and say—that the softest thing in the world is "as soft as the inside of a turtle might be"? Or the quietest "as quiet as a flea going to a dog"? And who but a young child would have the honesty to say, "Mother, I love you as much as peanut butter"?

Of course, one of the reasons the child's fresh images jostle us so is that they are sensory images, sprung from touch and taste, sharp seeing, smelling, feeling. Here again the child is a poet—though quite unself-consciously so. He is merely using the equipment that is his birthright; indeed, he has no other way to apprehend the world. But adult poets know that life in a poem springs from the use of lively senses. The poet John Hall Wheelock, for instance, reminds us that the kind of knowl-edge a poem offers is "a re-experience of the world in all its sensory and emotional impact."[1]

Two seven-year-olds peer at a mass of frog's eggs. Their comments delight us with their beautiful exactness; but, of course, what the boys are doing is merely observing closely, precisely, and bringing other senses to bear upon what they see. "It looks like they weave webs out of water." "Looks like a jellyfish that swallowed beads."

The same is true of this third-grade group description of a horned toad—a classroom pet:

> Prickly, soft-bottomed,
> eyes like black diamonds,

The horned toad scrambles
    along on his black-spotted
        stomach,
Stops, lifts his needle-horned
    Triceratops head,

Flattens out his snake skin-
    scaley, stripey self,

Shuffles along on pine-cone
    feet
Looking at the ground
With his eyes like
            Concord grapes,

Slips, slides, shoots along,

Dives into the gravel,
    and digs in
With his Stegosaurus
    tail.

The ten-year-old who wrote that his dog's fluffy paws "feel like miniature punching bags" surprises us with his lively tactile sense, and when we hear a seven-year-old say, "My cat runs like she is in a police car," we know that the child has indeed felt speed.

And here are some second-graders dictating to their teacher after a cold play period outdoors. The title of their story might be "What It Feels Like to Be Cold." I am tempted to say that only children this young can so easily find words and images to describe the physical sensations of cold.

Cold hands, skinny with lines
Nails hard from the cold
Lips ice dry
Wind that fights us
Noses that feel sticky with glue
Toes brick stiff
Cold tears, happy winter tears
So cold it hurts to breathe.

And here is a fifth-grader at the beach who has found a way to put into words a body sensation all of us have had, but few of us have ever tried to catch hold of, relish, and define:

As the waves come rolling
and roaring upon the beach
like hands grasping for food,
over my feet, over my knees,
I feel as if by some magic force
I'm running back, back and away,
even though I'm standing still
as a statue.[2]

The child is a poet, we have said, because his images are alive; he is bodily aware of the impact of his experiences; he reaches out with lively senses; and he is uninhibited by our conventions. Can we say also that his sensory receptivity and his lack of inhibition lie at the base of his playfulness? I am speaking of that playfulness which is one of the ingredients of poetry-making, essential in the whole approach to poetry; playfulness that leads to juggling with words, trying, testing, inventing.

Our preschool children are perhaps our greatest playful inventors. Here is an example of a four-year-old girl who, seeing a student teacher taking notes on the playground, approached and asked to dictate something. The playful words of nonsense, rhyme and strange reason that came pouring out may have been released by the fact that she was in a playful mood or felt that, since she was dictating, she was free—or perhaps even obliged—to move about among concepts that were symbols and words that were tinged with incantatory magic; in short, that it was up to her to make a poem. She experimented first with phrases that combined numbers and the names of letters and colors. Then came this short, delicate, completely playful and original construction:

E E for lunch
B B D D for brunch
A B Ho, Ho, Hop, hop;
A B C C
I E G G
A brunch
Six five three
H H   E E   G B.

Another child, this one a first-grader, plays with words and sounds suggesting to her the spookiness of Halloween. Though she may not have felt that she was dictating a poem—and indeed the teacher did not write it down in the shape of a poem— it is spoken in the playful spirit that can lead straight to poetry:

HALLOWEEN

Black cats, ghosts and goblins are
Halloween fun! Creaky houses are fun
too, oh boo! Halloween. Trick or
treat is said so much hush hush!
Scary costumes are worn so much.
Witches, pitches, little ditches!

Play with rhythm, too, leads to poetry; and all of us who have been around young children know very well how they chant rhythmically as they play; how they accompany their active games with rhythmic verbal formulas. "Eeny meeny miny mo, crack-a-feeny finy fo"—or its equivalent—rings out from every playground. It is as natural as breathing for children to love the regularly accented beat, in words and in actions. The poet Theodore Roethke, speaking of rhythm in poetry, has said that rhythm is a "clue to the energy of the psyche."[3] Isn't it true that the rhythmic, accented, playful verses that children both invent and learn so easily do indeed clue us in to the joyful, energetic state of being that belongs to early childhood?

I do not mean to claim that nursery chants and playground jump-rope rhymes are necessarily poetry. Yet many of them—including, of course, Mother Goose rhymes—suggest incantation and have intriguing combinations of sounds and rhythms that continue to delight us in adulthood and stay with us all our lives. No wonder the college student who repeated to me the following childhood rhyme had never forgotten it. It comes from the tobacco country in the South, where she grew up, and may have been influenced by the auctioneer's calls:

> Hey Bennie Rue
> And a Rue Bennie Bee
> And a Bee Bennie Thistle
> And a Ho Bennie Hustle
> And a little cut short.

But children are responsive also to other rhythms, not just those that beat rapidly in two-four time. They are able to find words that suggest the rhythmic quality of almost anything that moves—from trains to mice; and they easily write in any rhythm that appeals.

Today, of course, all of us are surrounded by a musical balladry peculiar to our time. The Beatles, the Monkees, Bob Dylan—children of all ages listen to these songsters, pick up the styles and the rhythms, and turn out their own versions of what they hear. I suggest that this is a legitimate "poetic" activity and can perhaps lead some children to a fullness of expression not possible for them through other channels. In the modern balladry they find a variety of rhythms and moods, along with the appeal of repetition. When a sixth-grade boy who is a low achiever can write a poem like the following, one can only feel grateful for the influences that have reached him and triggered such a sophisticated yet simple, rhythmic refrain:

SALLY AND TED

Sally has a doll that goes
Mom-mom, mom-mom, mom-mom.
Ted has a dog that goes
Bow-wow, Bow-wow, Bow-wow.
My father has a wife that goes
I love you, I love you,
I love you. And my sister
Has a boy friend that goes
Do you love me, Do you love me,
Do you love me? And my
Sister's boy friend has
A little sister that cries
and cries and cries.

Usually, though, when we speak of the child's facility with rhythms, I believe we are referring to his phenomenal ability simply to melt into the rhythm of whatever it is he is observing. He can make his words flow or jump or ripple—effort-lessly. A seven-year-old—possibly influenced by David McCord's "Grasshopper"—gives us her own version of the grasshopper's hop:

> A grasshopper
> was here and
> the grasshopper
> was there.
> And there he
> was   and
> here he was
>   here   here
>   there   there

And let me quote an eleven-year-old girl who has retained this ability to catch a rhythm and put it into words. (Often older children seem to lose the sensitivity and flexibility that would allow them to do this.) She begins with a proselike description of a tree in the wind, but then is caught up in the tree's rustling, playful, darting rhythm.

Actually, this piece of writing has a little of everything we have been referring to so far that is poetic in the language of childhood: it gives us playful metaphors, playful rhythm, im-ages of lively, glittering sight and whispering sound; and it is completely original, reflecting a child's own way of seeing, of being imaginative and enjoying, with no fears of what others will think of her.

TREES

> They sway in the wind as if they
> are about to snap but then all of a
> sudden it springs up like outstretched

arms reaching for the sun which glitters
and shines upon its many leaves like
a playful puppy darting in and out
sometimes hidden from view.
　　"Yet it is only a tree, only a
tree, only a tree, only a tree," whispers
the wind while it rustles the leaves.
"So, it can't be a puppy, can't be a puppy,"
echoes the wind. "Someday it may
be chopped down into firewood for some
lucky child, lucky child, lucky child,"
whispers the wind.

But let us remind ourselves at this point that poetry is more than rhythm and sound. In the beginning we spoke of the element of surprise in the child's fresh metaphors; of the delight we take in the unexpected likenesses they reveal. Wheelock would say that this is what poetry is mainly all about: "A poem is what happens when a poet rediscovers, for himself, the reality we have lost sight of because, to use Shelley's metaphor, it has been overlaid by the veil of familiarity."[4] We have said that the child's metaphors and similes are discovered by him in a natural way, as he attempts to connect the old with the new and build meanings through association. Perhaps we are the ones—rather than the children—who experience a sense of new awareness of old reality when we hear such thoughts as a seven-year-old's "black as a closed drawer" or "deep as a pot of soup for an ant."

Yet we know that even quite young children experience this joy of "rediscovering reality"—looking at the familiar world suddenly with a new insight. Here a seven-year-old boy surveys the ordinary city scene with a fine ability to reconstruct the past lying behind it. His language, perhaps, is not so poetic as his thought. Indeed, this is what happens when children begin to struggle with the act of putting very large thoughts into the small framework of language at their command:

A long time ago
Indians were everywhere you
    looked in the plains
    and in the woods.
And now everywhere
you look there are houses
    and houses.

Here an eight-year-old girl succeeds admirably in putting together a new thought about familiar birds and familiar planes:

BIRDS FLYING SOUTH

The winged beasts of the air
    that fly in V's and other shapes
go and come back. How gently they move.
    They seem to put the breeze in back of
                            their wings—
Not like the machines that fly among them.

I wonder if we encourage children enough to make discoveries like these. Do we share our own discoveries and insights with them? Do we read aloud to them the poets who successfully dig down beneath the layers of the familiar, in ways children can appreciate?

As I enter now this realm of discussion of the large thoughts of childhood, I am perhaps moving away from what we mean when we speak of the "poetic language of childhood." I am moving toward the very serious poems children of the middle years and older write to strengthen and discover their own identity; poems that help them deepen their capacity to deal with the world: poems often carrying such a burden of feeling that the words at the child's command can hardly support the weight of the thought. Such a poem is the following one on war, written by a nine-year-old girl. This child is leaving her childhood and standing at the threshold of adulthood. Her poem could serve as the prelude for another paper. I believe it is a fitting conclusion for the present discussion:

WAR

But why to kill a human body.
   To exchange thoughts,
and help each other.
   But just because the thoughts don't
latch, combine or go together
   Destroyed was blood, bone
brain that so carefully
put together make a human being.
But not just that have you destroyed
for God and Love still
stand in sorrow.

KARLA KUSKIN

KARLA KUSKIN, a poet and artist, has written and
illustrated 17 books for children. A native New
Yorker, Mrs. Kuskin lives in Brooklyn Heights
with her husband and their two children.

"Talk to Mice and Fireplugs . . ."

Did you ever see a lady
Who was walking down the street
With little laced old lady shoes
On stiff old lady feet?
Wispy haired and wrinkled
In pale, frail health
Talking tight old lady talk
To no one but herself.
Nodding and discussing
Beneath her dusty hat.
A child like me
Would not behave as foolishly as that.
I talk to mice and fireplugs
A toadstool
Or a tree
To bicycles
And bus stops
And they talk back to me. . . .
Hee hee.[1]

I read that verse to you because some of the lines explain
what I try to do when I write for children. I want to talk
through my verses to anyone: mice, fireplugs, assorted trees
and children, anyone who will listen. And I want to talk in

any voice: an old lady's, a child's, my cat's—in any voice that I choose to use. The children who hear my verses or read them to themselves will, hopefully, recognize a familiar feeling or thought. Or possibly an unfamiliar feeling or thought will intrigue them. If that spark is lit, then my verse may encourage its individual audience to add his own thought or maybe even a poem of his own, to try his own voice in some new way.

Like most people who write, I want to be heard and understood. A very direct way of finding out if someone out there is listening and if he understands is to read him what you have written. Whenever I finish writing something (it may even be a thank-you note), I read it aloud to my husband, my children and, if no one else is around, to myself and Rosalie Katskin, our Siamese cat.

The only way I know of getting the words out of my head and into the light is to try to meet them as you would a stranger and catch them unaware to learn how they *really* sound. Is the sense still there? Has an image collapsed? How does the silent reading differ from reading aloud? Does it work both ways? I've written a lot of verses that sounded splendid in a corner of my mind, but once they were echoing across the objective air, they lost their luster. They resemble those jewel-like stones you bring home from the beach on Sunday only to wonder on Tuesday why you brought home all those *stones*.

I am a firm believer in reading aloud because, I suppose, I loved it so much as a child. Both roles were wonderful—reader and listener. Truthfully I think that I liked reading best. It combines the advantage of listening to that fascinating sound —your own voice—with the feeling that whatever you were reading was a gift you were bringing to your audience. Because it was your discovery, you had part ownership. That's a marvelous feeling to have about T. S. Eliot's *Old Possum's Book of Practical Cats* or speeches from *A Midsummer Night's Dream*.

In the last dozen years I have often read my verses in quite a few different areas and to a variety of age groups, ranging from the pupils in private schools of New York City to children in inner-city schools of Washington, D.C. It's easy to read poetry to children who know and love poetry. It's very difficult to read to children who don't know what poetry is and care less.

Last spring I went to Washington, D.C., for a government agency called CAREL. That is the Central Atlantic Regional Educational Laboratory. Like most government agencies, its title is a veritable poem in itself. It was a terrible time to be in Washington or anywhere else. I made the trip on the morning Robert Kennedy died. The area I went to had suffered the worst effects of the rioting and destruction that erupted after the assassination of Martin Luther King a month before.

One of the schools I visited still had a good many windows broken. Its metal doors with their tiny chicken-wired windows were constructed to keep people out, not invite them in. Yet the children I read to were young and seemed completely unaffected by the current and terrible events. And for many of the older children, I suspect, the world had been hard enough, long enough so that they were not as surprised and shocked by the chaos as some of our more comfortable and better-protected citizens. Include me among the latter.

I first read to children of eight and nine years and realized quickly that they weren't with me. The poem I read was "The Witches Ride," which begins:

> Over the hills
> Where the edge of the light
> Deepens and darkens
> To ebony night,
> Narrow hats high

>Above yellow bead eyes
>The tatter-haired witches
>Ride through the skies. . . .[2]

A verse like that one—one that I would generally read to children of this age—just wasn't right. At the moment I didn't have time to figure out why. Instead, I had to do some quick experimenting to try to find a place where we could meet each other. I tried some shorter, funnier verses like:

WHEN I WENT OUT TO SEE THE SUN

>When I went out to see the sun
>There wasn't sun or anyone
>But there was only sand and sea
>And lots of rain that fell on me
>And where the rain and river met
>The water got completely wet.[3]

If a child laughs at what you say, he's listening; and he may keep listening even when you get a little more serious. I read my very shortest poem from a book called *Alexander Soames: His Poems*. The title is "Bugs."

>I am very fond of bugs.
>I kiss them
>And I give them hugs.[4]

The response should be poetic: *bugs . . . ugh(s?)*. I got the response. I also began to draw, fast and messy, but I wanted to hold attention. The words and the way they were put together may have been unfamiliar, but I hoped that the sketches would make the words plainer.

I read the first book I had written, *Roar and More,* and drew some of the animals. We were finally on common ground.

There were a great many requests for animals and for "a picture of me. . . . draw Ellie" and best of all "Let me draw," until we were all drawing together. *Roar and More* was effective here because the verses are short, simple and demand a response. Let me read a few:

> If a lion comes to visit
> Don't open your door
> Just firmly ask, "What is it?"
> And listen to him roar.
>
> ROAR![5]

> The elephant's nose makes a very good hose
> Or maybe a holder for flowers.
> It can snore, it can croon
> Or trumpet a tune.
> It has most remarkable powers.
>
> HOOOOONK[5]

> Fishes are finny
> Fishes are funny
> They don't go dancing
> They don't make money
> They live under water
> They don't have troubles
> And when they talk
> It looks like bubbles.
>
> OOOOO[5]

> The mouse runs up the halls
> And down the halls
> And into walls
> And out of walls
> He runs most anywhere he pleases

Searching for delicious cheeses.

eeep[5]

Giraffes don't huff or hoot or howl
They never grump, they never growl.
They never roar, they never riot,
They eat green leaves
And just keep quiet.[5]

Another book I have used is *Square as a House,* which is also in verse and which asks for a response quite directly. For example,

What would you choose
If you were free
To be anything fat
That you wanted to be?
Anything thin or long or tall,
Anything red, blue, black, at all:
A bird on the wing
A fish on the fin?
If you're ready to choose
It is time to begin.[6]

Which Horse Is William? does the same thing in prose. I told this story more than I read it. As with everything I read, I skipped freely and changed things if I thought they might seem too strange in their original form. This is the way I read the more flowery sections of *Wind in the Willows* to my son. Essentially, I am a great believer in using an unfamiliar word or phrase when it is called for, but when all the territory is unfamiliar, the going can get so discouraging that instead of gaining a questioner, you lose a listener.

The younger children I read to in these schools were very

alive, anxious to hear, to talk and to possess. They all wanted the drawings I was doing and were also fascinated with the idea of making or having a book of their own. If this had been an on-going program, I would have liked very much to work with some of them over a period of time on making their own books. Later some of these children did write poetry. (Some of it is reproduced below.)

I read very much the same kinds of poems to the older children that I had read to those who were younger. The older ones weren't as eager—perhaps the word is "free"—to talk, listen, take, give. I felt that a lot of them had been bored too long and had gotten used to not listening. They came around, but I had to work harder.

One of the things small children respond to first is rhythm as in clapping games and songs. Poems are tuneless songs. Beginning with short verses, using books that have built-in points for response, drawing pictures to hang ideas on or asking listeners to draw their own reactions while you are reading or when you have finished are all friendly ways of introducing poetry to a young child. With the phrase "young child," I am including all of those children who do not have a speaking— even a *nodding*—acquaintance with poetry.

The building materials of a poem are sound and the swing of it: words in their infinite color, length, shape, rhythm and, at times, rhyme. When they are used freely and impressionistically, a listener can enjoy the sound—just abstractly at first. Later he will listen to what is being said. "The Congo" by Vachel Lindsay is a drum solo. W. S. Gilbert's "When You're Lying Awake" from *Iolanthe* is a waterfall of words and silliness. "Jabberwocky" by Lewis Carroll is another handsome example of what the sound and roll of words can do. If we continue along this winsome road, we approach James Joyce country, where the terrain gets rougher.

However it is done—as formally as in a narrative poem like

"The Pied Piper of Hamlin" or "The Highwayman," as subtly
as in haiku or with the simplicity of some short descriptive
Emily Dickinson poetry—a poem is written to carry feeling
and thought. Usually the two are combined into a mood. Read-
ing both prose and poetry (even reading the back of the Sugar
Smacks Box) expands our private world and lets us in on
moods and lives that we are not familiar with. Through reading
we can become someone else anywhere else.

When I said before that I want to use different voices when
I write, I was referring to this kind of exploration of other lives.
If I can go into new thoughts and places in my imagination,
perhaps whoever is listening will follow. I do not wish to make
this sound more complicated than it is. Quite simply, I do not
spend all my days writing from the point of view of the New
York–born mother of two I am.

At times I would rather choose the voice of a child who only
speaks in rhyme:

> Once upon
> Upon a time
> There was a child
> Who spoke in rhyme.
> Three tall physicians and a nurse
> Have testified
> That it was verse.
> His hair was brown,
> His height was short.
> His pants were gray,
> The shorter sort.
> His name was Alexander Soames
> And when he spoke
> He spoke in poems.[7]

Or the voice of a snowman:

In the flaky frosty morning
some mittens made a start.
They rolled cold snow together
and they built my bottom part.
After that they made my middle
with pushes, slaps, and punches,
and then they left me headless
and went in to eat their lunches.[8]

I am working on a book now which pursues this theme.

How do I know if what I have written says what I want the way I want it to? By the reaction or lack of it. When a class of 30 children in Towson, Maryland, recited a poem of mine to me, I had two feelings. One, I wanted to become quietly invisible; and two, I knew my words had reached them from the way they muttered and roared them back at me. You know you have a good reaction when there is laughter, if you are trying to be funny and when there is an absorbed silence, if you are not. On occasions when my eight-year-old son suddenly quotes a few lines from something I have written or I overhear him reading a book of mine to his four-year-old sister, I momentarily feel that I have bridged that famous gap and said something both to them and me.

I want to add one thought here. Despite my pleasure when I am able to write something that communicates, I am, finally, not writing for my audience first, but for myself. In other words: if I don't think something is funny, I won't feel better about it if my son or a lot of other people's sons laugh at it. When it comes down to the crunch, as they say in *Time,* it is my feelings I finally have to trust.

But I was talking about children's reactions to reading. One of the very best of these happens when a child listens for awhile and then is inspired to take up his own pencil and write. Then you know that he has enjoyed what he's heard or read so much that he wants to create some of the same. It may also mean that he wasn't entirely satisfied and thinks he can do better. Sometimes he's right.

Certainly the most precious thing about each of us is that which makes us different—the private view, imagination, voice that in some small way is our own and belongs to nobody else. Writing, painting, all the arts are products of this voice or view. When young children write poetry, when children who have not heard much poetry write, they are still free. They have not learned the rules and restrictions. Such work is comparable to the wonderful paintings done by talented children before they are taught *how* to draw and use perspective.

These few poems were written by the children at the Madison School in Washington, D.C., after they were visited by several writers including myself. The children are speaking in poetry:

> Grass: in the house
>   my feet
> are
>   green
>
> Bird
>   is a dark
> place
>   for singing
> safe
>   from
>   rain
>
>   death:
>   something
> calls
>   you down

Reading and writing encourage each other. Once you want to write, you read more. In each way, that private world of knowledge and feeling is expanded.

I will tell you one more reaction that I have had to my work. About two years ago, when Nicholas Kuskin was six years old, I was reading *Alexander Soames* to him.

I began at the beginning and continued with the tale of the boy who always spoke in poems:

> The first time Alex saw a cat
> He did not run,
> He simply sat
> And said,
> "It's flat
> That that's
> A cat."
>
> And when he saw a dog he said,
> Scratching his small poetic head,
> "The walk of a dog
> Is more of a jog
> And less of a dance
> Than the amble of ants."
>
> . . .
> Alexander Sandwich Soames
> Wrote these verses, rhymes, and poems.[9]

When I came to those last two lines, my son laughed loudly and said, "You make money writing that?" That's the thing about wanting to be heard—you have to take the consequences.

NANCY LARRICK

Poetry in the Classroom

Somebody asked me what textbook I used in my poetry workshop at Lehigh University's School of Education. The answer was "None," and the answer will always be the same. The teachers who enroll for the workshop are urged, however, to read as much poetry as they possibly can. And they are encouraged to learn more about poetry from the children they teach.

Classroom happenings and classroom poetry are reported at every session. There may be only a score of teachers in the workshop, but I get a feeling that the participants number about 500.

The new poetry surge is not limited, of course, to the Lehigh Valley. In countless classrooms across the country, from kindergarten up, children are reading, chanting or singing poetry more than ever before. Many are writing poetry as naturally as they talk.

Teachers are emphasizing pleasure, not conformity. Concentration on metrical patterns and rhyme schemes, which used to vivisect verse in earlier generations, has almost disappeared. The child is encouraged to see and dream and feel as a poet does. Once he begins to develop his talent, he feels good about poetry—and often about reading in general.

The child's love of singing poems has led teachers to begin with musical Mother Goose rhymes and folksongs. The old songs and their modern counterparts invite every child to get into the act, by singing, by clapping and by improvising with new words.

Pete Seeger asks his listeners to join him in his recordings, *American Folk Songs for Children* and *Bought Me a Cat and Other Animal Folk Songs* (available from Folkways Scholastic Records). Children sing, "Little bird, little bird, fly through my window." Then Seeger tells them to invent stanzas bringing their own heroes through their windows.

The old folksong "She'll Be Comin' Round the Mountain" inspired some ten-year-olds to sing, "She'll be wearin' a miniskirt when she comes, wow-wow!", "She'll be wearin' a red bikini when she comes, yip-pee!" and, in funereal tones, "She'll be ridin' in a hearse when she goes, boo-hoo!"

Poetry begins when a child learns how to see the world around him. Even such familiar items as a piece of string or a wet leaf on a sidewalk are worthy of notice. A few questions from the teacher (or from a poetically aware parent) may start the child thinking: "What does it look like? How does it make you feel?"

Once they begin to observe carefully, children come up with comments that are the stuff of poetry. To an eight-year-old, an olive shell is "a submarine sailing through the sea." To another, "A daisy is a ballerina/The petals go up and down."

Aileen Fisher gives a fine example of how children may feel about ordinary things. In her poem *I Like Weather,* she says, "I like it when it's mizzly and just a little drizzly . . . I like it when it's foggy and sounding very froggy."

Few children can equal Miss Fisher's talent, but they are moving right along. Thus a fifth-grader wrote, "The lightning is a giant's flashlight," and a second-grader said, "The fog is a monster eating up buildings and houses." A third-grader's concept was, "Fog is walking to nowhere without a sidewalk."

Children like colors as much as they like fresh paint. Some are astonished to learn that red isn't necessarily red all over. There is the red of cherries, tomatoes, strawberries, beets, radishes, fire engines, and the necktie that Daddy has worn only once since Christmas. "Orange is a fish swimming in the water/singing a song of long ago," a fourth-grader wrote. "Gray feels like a lost kitten whose fur is cold and wet," said another.

Joan Walsh Anglund's book *What Color Is Love?* (Harcourt) is particularly evocative. After reading it to her three children, one young mother asked, "Well, what color is love?"

Jessie, five and a half, said, "Gold is love."

David, eight and a half, replied, "But love is not gold./It is shiny money-color/and a crust of bread."

Daniel, seven, said, "But gold is a color."

David replied, "And love is real."

Jessie summed up, "When I'm happy, I feel gold, because I'm a goldfish."

David concluded, "When I'm happy, I feel yellow, because I think of the sun and I'm bright inside."

Group enthusiasm captured a batch of five-year-olds when they walked across the Lehigh River bridge and through part of the Bethlehem Steel Company's plant. When they got back to their classroom, they dictated a group poem:

> The steel mill is like a big bear
> behind steel bars.
> High, high buildings . . .
> As big as a Ferris wheel going around
> Like an apartment house smoking.

At night it is all lit up
And blinking like a giant's castle.
Fire is coming out
Cement is gushing through a pipe
and big stacks are smoking.

It feels hot! It feels hot to look at!
Yellow coal
red coal
white coal.
Water in the canal shows colors
of a big red fire.
The steel mill makes red windows in the water
Red and orange lights shine on colored water
flashing lights and color like lightning
The work sounds like thunder.

When I see the steel mill I feel strong
like a working truck.

When the teacher read aloud the collective poem, the children asked for a tape recording. This was made. Then it was edited and reedited until all of the authors were satisfied. As one child explained, "It's a poem, so it's got to be right."

Once children see that their poetic language is welcomed, they become more and more imaginative. Here are some thoughts of six-year-olds, quoted in my anthology *Green Is Like a Meadow of Grass* (Garrard):

Rain taps on your windows
Giants running on the clouds
Flashing their flashlights.

Rain in the street
Like a lake for ants.

Rain on the grass
Like a machine gun.

Thunder is a running horse.

Thunder is giants bowling.
When it lightens
A giant gets a strike.

Rain on the windows
Like silver stones,
Like bullets
Heading toward your windshield,
Like silver dots on the glass,
Like people walking tippytoe
On your car roof.

When rain drops on flowers
It makes a little noise
Like a ladybug walking on grass.

Printed on a long scroll of shelf paper and hung on the wall, "Rain" became the best-loved reading matter of its composers—some of whom had never gone beyond the banalities of Dick and Jane. "It's ours, you see," one of the children said.

The same youngsters showed a lively interest in the work of published poets. They were not bothered by unrhymed verses. They enjoyed haiku and other Oriental patterns. And they especially liked the humor of John Ciardi, as exemplified in

"Mummie Slept Late and Daddy Cooked Breakfast" from *You Read to Me, I'll Read to You* (Lippincott). Daddy's waffle was like "a manhole cover" and Daddy's child concludes:

> I think I'll skip the waffles.
> I'd sooner eat the plate.

Another poet who is popular with the young is David McCord. These lines are from *Every Time I Climb a Tree* (Little, Brown):

> Every time I climb a tree
> I scrape a leg
> Or skin a knee
> . . .
> Though climbing may be good for ants
> It isn't awfully good for pants
> But still it's pretty good for me
> Every time I climb a tree.

Like other modern poets who write for children, David McCord keeps his emotions pitched low—and this understatement makes his recorded readings all the more effective. Children want to be stirred, but without any fuss and without any syrup, thank you. They respond instantly to *Prayers from the Ark* (Viking) by the French poet Carmen Bernos de Gasztold. These short poems, written primarily for adults, are the prayers of Noah's passengers. The ox prays for time to be unhurried, the mouse wants to be unspied upon, the monkey hopes someday to be taken seriously, the ducks ask for "plenty of slugs and other luscious things to eat." After hearing these prayers, hundreds of children have written their own prayers for members of Noah's menagerie. Some of these have been exceptionally fine.

Not all children prefer the same poems, of course, and a child's taste may differ sharply from an adult's. The goal is to let each child develop such a liking for poetry that he will search for it wherever he goes.

JUNE JORDAN

JUNE JORDAN was born in Harlem and grew up in
Bedford-Stuyvesant, Brooklyn. She has taught at the
City College of New York, Connecticut College and
Sarah Lawrence. Her publications include a book-
length poem of black American life, *Who Look at
Me,* and an anthology of black American poetry.

Children and
the Hungering For

Let me tell you about poetry as something natural. Let me
show you how poetry, how the hungering for metaphors in-
finitely based on you and me, is more natural than everyday
dialog. If you will believe me, maybe more of us can affirm
the human purpose of poetry.

All of us hunger a great part of our public and secret time,
alive. We reach and we dream, we surmise and we concentrate
beyond the limits of ourselves. Or we scheme against the facts
of isolation. We hope for love. We even memorize an enormous
store of data merely on the premise that someday our lives
will join that knowledge, to good purpose.

People look for coalitions or they laboriously construct a
cultural identity larger than their own. Being alone appears to
be a problem. Everywhere you find the evidence of human
longing to coincide, to blur individual boundaries.

Our obsession to overcome separation stems from a primary
perception of essential loneliness. The first knowing of oneself,
as alone, is painful and early. It occurs in the context of
mother and child. Recognition of the Other, of non-self, can-
not be avoided. Nor can we evade the pain of initial separation;

when the infant separates from his parent, he loses his safety. Distinction between the identities of mother and child lead the child into vulnerable experience. None of us ever learns to dissociate pain from separation, entirely.

Adults carry around a hunger born of limited relationship. But the years obscure the original awareness of safe dependency, and the hunger loses its outward momentum. When they grow up, people begin to talk about things missing inside themselves rather than the issues, the other lives, they have failed to positively intersect. To grow old often means to turn away and to worry about one's navel, with more and more despair. (One's navel cannot compare with the world, no matter who you are.)

Since the newborn person is necessarily a student, and since children are necessarily close to the first trauma of limited relationship, they embody *a hungering for:* Children fill their lives with learning: they hurtle themselves outward, into the greater reality, hoping to embrace, without perishing.

At its best, poetry records the self in positive intersection with someone else, or with outside circumstance. Poetry engulfs reality in a communicating form. In fact, apprehension through poetry is valid because it communicates: poetry is valid because it includes beyond the self.

Poetry is your own naming of the world. As such, it provides relief from the hazards of dependency. Rather than simply accepting terms—this is a *table,* this is *downstairs*—the poet chooses, he determines the names of his universe.

As your own naming of the world, poetry protects your independence from the frightening implications of limit. Poetry serves an independence of power and privilege. Rather than the independence of the forsaken, or the victim, or the weak, poetry asserts the personal freedom of definition and synthesis. Poetry supports the prerogative of the always only one: the self confronting the other, in a manner that will generate healthy control of the communion, i.e., control endangering no aspect, nor any factor, in the assimilating process.

Poetry confers the power and the privilege of independence as a condition purged from threats to survival.

In psychoanalytic literature, we read that the human capacity to risk embrace, the capacity to trust, depends upon the nature of the first relationship, and its rupture. Since the break, or the bifurcation of identities seldom takes place without hurt and fear, we commonly link isolation with death.

The process of poetry, profoundly treats with the difficult awareness of being alone. Poetry directly calms the anxiety attending separate position. For poetry overcomes the subject to object relationship. Poetry triumphs over the separation; in its place, a poem will invent relationship. Objects become parts of the subject, they enlarge the developing self. In poetry, objects are reclaimed by the subject from the Realm of the Other to the Realm of My Self.

We may usefully think about the coincidence between the time when children begin their so-called "mastering of sentences" and the normal timing of the child's perception of his mother as a distinctive entity. The coincidence translates as follows: Child, or subject, recognizes his mother as separate, or as object, even as the child begins talking in sentences. Here it helps to remember that mastering sentences actually means adoption of the subject versus object system of thought.

From the moment of this coincidence, onward, poetry poses an urgent liberation for all children: it presents an opportunity to control the meaning of separation, or to obliterate separation and to enmesh and to enrich enmeshed realities through simile, metaphor, and association of sounds.

In its contemporary emergence, poetry declares our freedom

from the regimentation of grammar and syntax; poetry under-
girds the desiring areas of I and Thou acknowledgment.

The creative retrieval of erstwhile objects, and/or the hur-
dling of fearful separation, mightily meets the child's hungering
for. In poetry, the retrieval of objects signifies the organic,
the growing integration of reality with self.

Accordingly, the poem is affirmative as well as therapeutic,
for the individual. And it is inherently humane: Poetry is not
objective; it is governed by moral values and the instinctual
blurring of limitation.

For more than three years, I have been privileged to test
these assumptions about poetry, with children. The Academy
of American Poets has sent me into New York City public
schools serving every age level and income level and racial mix
or racial segregation.

After reading some of my poetry, and the poetry of people
I admire, we talk. Let me share a couple of events I clearly
remember.

At one school, the kids asked me about this poem:

THIS MAN

This old whistle
could not blow
except
to whiskey wheeze
with bandage on his head
temple to temple
black
and dry hands
in his pockets keeping
warm
two trembling fists

clammed
against a stranger
('s) blueandwhite sedan
he
would never drive
could not repair
but damaged
just by standing there.

So I explained: I saw this man standing outside my window, and he watched me watching him, for almost an hour. Finally, I left the windowsill and wrote the poem. Why? Otherwise, I might forget about him. Why does it rhyme? Because I wanted the reader to remember the poem: remember This Man.

That seemed to make sense to them. They wanted to try remembering, in poetry.

In a Harlem elementary school, the students sat so quietly, I felt uncomfortable. So, after a few minutes of zig-zag through already written poetry, I suggested that we write poetry together. They were not enthusiastic. On the board, I wrote: "RISE LIKE LIONS AFTER SLUMBER." They liked that line. And they agreed to assemble themselves in pairs: Taking that as the first line, one student would compose the next, and his partner would provide the clincher. The pairs kept changing composition and the chairs kept changing their position, and the verses they composed were very enjoyable, as a matter of fact.

At the High School of Fashion Industries, a girl challenged me: How come your poems are so simple? (What do you mean?) Don't you ever write allegory? (What's an allegory?) She explained, and I listened. Then I told her how I try to write a poetry that will reach people right away. If they want to, later, they can read it again and perhaps the poem will spread, thicken, or seem unintelligible. But right away, I want to reach people and let them share my words with me. In the next period, she sneaked back to tell me about the non-allegorical poetry she'd been piling up, for months. She had been afraid her poetry was "too direct."

Out on Governor's Island, in New York, mostly white children, by turning around in a full circle, can see Manhattan's skyline, trees, horizon, the river running into the ocean, men in military uniform, and semi-civilian institutions like their public school. I went there and found the students excited to hear the poetry of black, inner-city youngsters. Soon they were engaged in a fantasy: Suppose I'm black and suppose the grass is hard enough to kill you, if you slip. Suppose the whole block looks like a long, big, angry stone. What would I write? They tried, they wrote and, at last, we decided on a different project. The children wanted to invite black poets, of their own age, over to the island: they could eat lunch and then they could eat poems, together: Write them together. Thus, the adult witnesses to this idea tried, and wrote, and telephoned each other, but The Board of Education, and its various regulations, prevailed. Nevertheless, the young black poets and their waiting friends remain, in willingness.

Throughout the city schools, I met children who were eager to grasp anything usable. Poetry is usable. And I met children eager to expand and multiply relationships; poetry starts the multiplication of relationships.

> Now, there's a place in the city where the
> children don't sleep. Not well, and not long
> enough, any night.
> There's a place in the city where the children
> don't eat. Not well, and not often enough.
> There's a place in the city where the children
> have to hide

have to lie
have to fight
and sometimes have to kill
      It is not a slum
      It is not a ghetto.
      It's not even a community.
'It's blocked-in kids next to each other, and others and others.
      It's no particular stairway.
      It's violent isolation.
      It's violent loneliness.
      It's a place in the city some children call home.

You can find these children in the Fort Greene section of Brooklyn, which is across the bridge, or across two bridges, or three bridges, from Manhattan. But once you get inside Fort Greene, you might as well forget about the bridge. There are no bridges leading the children from Fort Greene to some-place else.

About a year and a half ago, a small group of black and Puerto Rican youngsters stood together in Fort Greene, on a Saturday morning. Where they stood was cold. They were try-ing to get into somewhere: somewhere warm with chairs and a table and a couple of lights.

A white teacher, Terri Bush, and myself, stood with these children, and finally they got into someplace else: somewhere of their own.

The Church of the Open Door let this group meet weekly in a large and sometimes sunny room. There we collaborated to bring books, records, snack stuff, paper and pencils. After a free while of dancing, book browsing and gossip, the kids would take a title, one they individually accepted, and write a poem, an editorial, an essay, a story, a fable, a joke. The lack-ing structure of our Workshop reflected a deliberate attempt to emphasize the separation between Saturdays and school, which is a place where children "fail." At the same time, we tried to obliterate the usual distinctions between creative writing, or art, and life. We were trying to prove, by having it happen, that poetry is as natural as neighborhood friends and as natural as dancing the Funky Four Corners.

Within a few months, the original group increased in size and in its commitment. The children elected to form a magazine called *The Voice of the Children.*

Now they were publishing, once a week. The second sight of their work, changed into type, transmuted from a private to a more public (legible) statement, tremendously excited the kids. In addition, when they were able to read their writings, in typescript, they became critical, in new ways, and their craft rapidly advanced. As, and only if, requested by the children, their published work changed with respect to spelling. No inflections were added, nor was any idiomatic usage "corrected." From the habitual and building fluency of their work, the children, spontaneously, became concerned about punctuation, stanzas, paragraphs, and form, generally. Questions about these technicalities were pursued by the children because they wanted to make sure that what they said could not be mistaken, by anybody.

Today, the audience that admires the children's work has widened even as the distinction and clarifying moment of their voices steadily deepens. The very experience of successful communication has assisted the children in their constructive overleaping of poverty-limitations. And their valuable awareness of special identity has been strengthened.

Who are these twelve- to fifteen-year-olds? They are supposedly represented in the charts that everywhere describe impoverished youngsters as inarticulate, verbally deficient, and intractable/unresponsive.

Listen to some of their voices. I would like to begin with

the poetry of Michael Goode, aged from twelve to thirteen since last year when he wrote this poem, on the evening of April fourth. A number of the children were together, that night, on their way to a poetry reading, when they learned that Martin Luther King had been shot. Among themselves, they abruptly spoke their terror: *Might as well die. There's going to be war. We'll lose. Might as well fight and die. Run to a cave. A cave would be too boring. Better to fight and then to die.* Just before the poetry reading began, it was learned that Dr. King had died. While the older poets read their poems, on that night, Michael Goode wrote his own:

APRIL 4, 1968
by Michael Goode (*twelve years old*)

war war
why do god's children fight among each other
like animals
a great man once lived
a Negro man
his name was the Rev. Martin Luther King.
but do you know what happened
he was assassinated by a white man
a man of such knowledge as he
Martin Luther King
a man of such courage
to stand up and let a man hit him
without hitting back.

yes
that's courage
when you fight back of course you're brave
but do you think you yourself

can stand up
and let someone beat you
without batting an eyelash
that takes courage.

shot him down
that's right
one of god's children

well you can count on a long hot summer
one of our black leaders has been killed
murdered
down into the gutter

I will long remember this dark day.

it's funny it's so you can't even
walk out in the street anymore
some maniac might shoot you
in cold blood.

what kind of a world is this?

I don't know.

Here are two other poems by Michael Goode:

TALKING

Some people talk in the hall
Some people talk in a drawl
Some people talk, talk, talk
And never say anything at all.

ADDITION PROBLEM

MOTHER	FATHER
WIFE	CHILD
SERGEANT	PRESIDENT
MINUTES	HOURS
DAYS	WEEKS
MONTHS	YEARS
HELL	HEAVEN
U.S.O.	U.S.A.
FRIENDS	ENEMIES
CRITICAL	DYING
GOING	GONE

WAR

These are a couple of poems by Carlton Minor:

DEW

The flowers dance
   in the warm
   sunlight
And the sun is
   blocked by the
   cloud
Then the sun
   breaks free of its
   enemies
And shines on the
   dancing flowers.
As the dew drops
   gleam
Like sparkling
   diamonds
   on

Arabian
fingers.

THE ROARING WIND

The wind blow on the sea
as the wind over the land russle the leaves
the animals roam the golden shores
waiting for the thunder to roar
when it roars the animals flee
    like a dog
    that is
    getting
    bit
    by
    fleas.

This is a poem by my son, who also attends the Workshop:

I'VE SEEN ENOUGH

I've been through Africa
I was there when Solomon was claimed king
I was best man to Cleopatra
I've seen the death of a million men in Japan
When that treacherous bomb was dropped
Surely I can say I've seen enough
What more proof need I tell you?
Must I tell you that I bore the cross
On which Jesus Christ was crucified?
Jesus Christ! I tell you surely
I've seen enough.

Poem by Deborah Crawford:

I will never, never in my long life
be a big head lady with a big head husband

I will never in my life be a millionaire
with a millionaire son and a millionaire cat

I will never in all my days be a poor lady with
a poor child and a poor aunt

I will never never in my life be a teacher with
a bald head boy friend.

Poem by Anthony Holmes:

DARKLING AFTERNOON

The afternoon is dark
The trees are blowing
the streets are clear
the sun is nowhere in sight
after a long cold night.

Poem by Juanita Bryant:

MY LIFE

My life is just a dream
That wonders all the time
Sometimes it goes into a shell
But it is hard to come out
My life My life
What have I done to you
You're wasting away
What shall I do?
Shall I dream
Or shall I scream
What shall I do
My life My life.

Poem by Michael Gill:

> The Jazz world
> Full of colors
> Flashing popping
> Coming from everywhere
> Jazz is Love
> Coming from the inner mine
> Sweet and soft
> I wish Jazz was
> here
>   All
>   The Time

Poem by Glen Thompson:

> THE AIR IS DIRTY,
> THE STREETS ARE DIRTY,
> THE WATER IS DIRTY,
> HALF THE PEOPLE ARE DIRTY,
> YOU CALL THIS LIVING?
>
> YOU SEE THE UGLY HOUSES,
> YOU BREATHE THE UGLY AIR,
> YOU WALK THE UGLY STREETS,
> YOU HEAR THE UGLY NOISES,
> AND CALL IT LIVING?
>
> YOU CAN CALL IT LIVING IF YOU LIKE,
> BUT I DON'T DIG IT AND I'M GOING TO
> SPLIT FROM IT AND I'M GOING TO
>
> BREATHE FRESH AIR,
> WALK CLEAN STREETS,

MEET GOOD FRIENDS,
LISTEN TO SWEET SOUNDS,
AND LIVE, LIVE, LIVE

Because the Voice of the Children's Workshop springs from a collaboration between a public school teacher of English, and myself, we have been concerned to imagine, at least, how Saturdays could take place in the classroom.

I wish all periods of study included poetry as the personal summary and evaluation of the hour that has passed.

I wish every public school system would imitate the poetry program devised by The Academy of American Poets: This would mean the developing of alliances between poets and schools. Kids would come into contact with people who mainly play or battle with words, *for their lives*. Older poets would eventually discover their younger counterparts, and these young poets could guide after-school workshops, in their neighborhoods.

As for the English classroom, let me recommend the organizing of a browsing situation, wherever possible: browsing research, browsing reader periods. Engage each class in an exploration of the range of poetry and then, in the last half of a semester, pursue a consensus curriculum, together. Challenge the children to find the materials for poem-to-newspaper-item-to-essay-to-short-story comparisons: What's the impact, and why? How does the writer/poet convince and involve you? I don't think comparisons will yield much excitement unless the children truly and freely find their own materials.

Browsing and comparison provide for creative relationship.

I began by talking about poetry and the separation that takes place between every mother and every child. Two weeks ago, fifteen-year-old Linda, editor-in-chief of *The Voice of the Children,* had to leave her home and her mother. She had to separate from her mother, permanently. She had to separate from her mother in order to stop the violence of no love. She had to cancel a first relationship. While the Welfare Department has been arranging a new shelter for Linda, she has been dealing with this separation. Let me close with her poems, written during the last ten days:

Poetry by Linda X:

> My joy is a thing of the past
> How did I get
>   here   and who am I
> I'm trading a dream
> My tears peacefully sleeping
> My lips unable to move
> While I wait my self becomes
>   my future
> For the lord is my Shepherd
>   And I'm looking to find him

. . .

> When you burn you earn your
>   place in the world
> When you're living your life is
>   like
> a lonely chair in an only room
> When you're dead you're the hero
>   of the world
> And you are forgotten you use to
> existed   The End.

. . .

> While I wait myself becomes my future fate
> up in the air I flow away

my destination is unknown
Home memory roll it up
   throw it away
for I am motherless another
        day

      .   .   .

the grey sky
  the bare
    street
    what has life meant
   to me

It has meant
  brutality
  pain
  ignorance
  pain
  crying
  pain
  wars
  pain
  death
  pain
  life
  pain
I saw the grey sky and the bare streets

It's Not a Joyous City

Jean Wilkinson, a teacher in California, asked me to listen to a tape recording made by an inner-city boy who had spurned reading until he met a poem that caught his interest. I heard a husky young voice, hamming up the simple lines of a poem by Gwendolyn Brooks, "We Real Cool":

THE POOL PLAYERS
SEVEN AT THE GOLDEN SHOVEL

> We real cool. We
> Left school. We
> Lurk late. We
> Strike straight. We
> Sing sin. We
> Thin gin. We
> Jazz June. We
> Die soon.[1]

If this was what "nonreaders" were reading, I decided I'd better spend some time in inner-city schools and see for myself, hopefully as a participating teacher.

My first visit was to a junior high school in an old building in inner-city Philadelphia—forbidding, ominous, prison-like, as are many schools of its vintage. On the way to the third floor, I observed near chaos in the corridors, with pupils running and shouting and pushing. The English teacher who was my guide explained that a few days ago there had been a stabbing on the school steps which eighth-graders watched as though it were a ball game.

After this preparation, my experience was rather mild. Nonetheless I was shaken at being in a classroom of 30 or 35 youngsters where there was no quiet for even a second. Nor was there a moment when everyone was sitting or standing still. There was constant talking, punching, running around, singing out.

The class reminded me of the shouted comment of a youngster in the Manhattan Country School which I had visited shortly before. A little Negro girl, obviously defiant over something that had happened earlier, suddenly cried out, "Well, that's what they tell me—if you can't join 'em, beat 'em." She probably spoke for many inner-city youngsters.

Somehow I put across the purpose of my Philadelphia visit: to get help in selecting poetry for a book which would be published. This was such a new idea that it did bring near silence. No one had ever said to these students, "*You* tell *me* what is good by your standards." I persuaded each to get a partner, to sit down, and to read the packets of poetry I had brought. Immediately the running commentary was resumed.

"Aren't there any poems about gangsters? I want a poem about gangsters."

Somebody else said, "Yes. Air pollution. Why aren't there any poems about air pollution?" And so it went. At first I was a little nonplussed by these questions. Finally I said to the young man who had asked about gangsters, "I haven't any poem about present-day gangsters, but I have some about pirates." No, he wanted gangsters now. So I said, "How about writing one?" And he did immediately.

Despite the constant hubbub and confusion, I was able to make the rounds from one pair to another. Their questions were very perceptive.

Those youngsters had a gift for putting their finger on a word or phrase which needed interpretation. For example, they asked the meaning of "deferred" in the first line of the poem

"Harlem" by Langston Hughes: "What happens to a dream deferred?" Then I realized that with the present generation "deferred" is used only in connection with the draft. No wonder they asked, "How can a dream be deferred?"

When it came to listing favorite poems, Langston Hughes' poetry led all the rest, with Carl Sandburg's a close second. Such poems as "Mother to Son" and "Harlem" by Hughes were immediate favorites. Also popular were the poems of Charles Reznikoff, Gregory Corso, Ferlinghetti, some poems of May Swenson and Eve Merriam, a couple of old poems of E. B. White, such as "Dog Around the Block," which they thought was just great, a few poems of Patricia Hubbell about construction and city scenes, and one or two poems written by youngsters in the Freedom Schools of Georgia in 1965.

The poems they chose are not the ones we usually think of as appropriate for children. Some of the Eve Merriam and Patricia Hubbell poems were written for children; the rest had been published for adults.

A second inner-city school that I visited is also in an old building, but it has been transformed by new lighting, new paint, and a great deal of wall-to-wall carpeting. It has an excellent school library and broadcasting studio.

I met first with fifth-graders and later with eighth-graders in the sprawling Learning Center, which has multicolored chairs and tables, bookcases, audiovisual equipment, and so on. We finally agreed we could read poetry better if we got closer together. So we sat on the floor, elbow to elbow. I can't imagine a more relaxed, interesting and really exciting group of people to sit down with for a poetry session.

In this group only one person spoke at a time, although there were quick interruptions from the others. The comments were far more philosophical than in the other school, but it is easier to be philosophical when you are sitting cross-legged on a carpeted floor.

I had brought a little poem by Langston Hughes which is a favorite of mine:

> In the morning the city
> Spreads its wings
> Making a song
> In stone that sings.
>
> In the evening the city
> Goes to bed
> Hanging lights
> About its head.[2]

I had thought a good title for the book would be *The City Spreads Its Wings*. But one girl said immediately that wouldn't do at all, and her classmates agreed. When I asked why, I was told, "Because it's talking about a joyous city." Another youngster said, "Of course it is." "But Philadelphia is not a joyous city," came the rejoinder, "and you know it." The discussion ended, and I chose another title.

Several youngsters wished to tell me that they, too, had written poems. My young friend who wanted a poem about gangsters wrote a poem while I was in his chaotic class.

A ninth-grade inner-city boy gave the following poem to a neighbor—not his own teacher—and it eventually came to me. The title: "Is God Dead?"

> Is God dead?
> He could be vacationing.
> Or could He be selling flowers at the
>   corner of Germantown and Penn?
> Maybe He's visiting a shrink.
> Or could He be in your living room,
>   wagging His tail,
> When you come home from a hard day's teaching?
> Maybe He's in jail for starting a riot.

Or figuring a way to peace for a war
   He didn't start.
Where is God? Is God dead?

—MARTIN RADCLIFFE[3]

As these city youngsters named favorite poems, their first choice turned out to be a poem that had appeared in *Negro Digest*. It is by Evelyn Tooley Hunt and is entitled "Taught Me Purple":

> My mother taught me purple
>   Although she never wore it.
> Wash-gray was her circle,
>   The tenement her orbit.
>
> My mother taught me golden
>   And held me up to see it,
> Above the broken molding,
>   Beyond the filthy street.
>
> My mother reached for beauty
>   And for its lack she died,
> Who knew so much of duty
>   She could not teach me pride.[4]

Many children I met, and hundreds of thousands in the same situation, are those whose mothers taught them purple, but did not teach them pride. Like Langston Hughes in the poem "Harlem," theirs is a "dream deferred," drying up "like a raisin in the sun."

Poetry sings to these children as it does to all children. When the emotional involvement is in harmony with their experience, they embrace the joy of seeking and creating. And this, I think, is the goal of all reading; indeed, of all education. I believe it is what poetry is doing for children today.

A DISCUSSION LED BY

WARREN DOTY and SAMUEL ROBINSON

WITH THEIR STUDENTS:
ROMANI WARDLAW, VERONICA WEST,
JUAN DAWSON AND JAMES HEATH

WARREN DOTY and SAMUEL ROBINSON are English
teachers at Simon Gratz High School in Philadelphia.
Students on the panel are juniors and seniors at
Simon Gratz, now an all-black high school of the
inner-city.

Straight Talk From Teenagers

MR. ROBINSON: We are going to combine the reading of poetry
by the students with spontaneous discussion. We've met once
or twice informally and discussed our views of poetry in the
classroom. But we felt that we didn't want to have a formal
presentation. So what you'll be seeing will be done for the first
time.

I'd like to emphasize that these students will be acting as
teachers. That means that you will be acting as students. We
encourage you to ask questions, interrupt as you would want
students to ask questions. In fact, our presentation demands
that you ask questions.

We will begin with the reading of several poems by a stu-
dent who asks that we not identify her by name. The first:

Who knows from whence I came?
Who knows my name?

I cannot think for myself because
I have a feeling I'm someone else.
Someone tell me why I'm without
a name!
Someone tell me why I feel so ashamed.
Was my name always like this?
Meaningless?
Or, did someone take it from me in punishment?
There's only one girl that I cannot understand,
I am that girl, for I know not who I am.

The second is self-explanatory:

I want what I get not,
I get what I want not,
I know what I need not,
And I want what I have not.

MR. DOTY: Many young poets are concerned about personal identity, but I wonder if we can find what motivates them. What encourages them to write down their wonderings and their anxieties?

When I put these questions to this girl, she replied:

"I just wrote it when the thought hit me. I had words going through my mind, and they came out on paper. It just happened naturally."

MR. ROBINSON: How can we encourage this naturalness in school?

VERONICA: I feel that this poem could be encouraged in life because as far as the black person is concerned, who knows really from whence we came? You separated us, our tribes. Who knows from whence we came? Who knows my name? My tribe's name, my people's name. You separated us when you brought us over. I cannot think for myself; society thinks for me. You have many rules. If I don't conform to these rules, I am breaking society's laws. I cannot think for myself. I have a feeling I'm someone else.

MR. DOTY: Do you think these kinds of feelings are often expressed by students in the classrooms you know?

VERONICA: Maybe not in poetry, but people have always had ways of saying different things. They take action or meditate or just sit down and wonder. And others write.

MR. ROBINSON: Is this encouraged or discouraged by other teachers?

JUAN: I'd like to say it is encouraged only in a phony sense. The teachers wave Shakespeare in the student's face, but students are not identifying at all. It's a whole confused thing. And then teachers tell the student, "Write a poem today in class." You write a poem or get an F. You can't force poetry on people. You can't tell them, "Sit down and write." You got to let them sit down and do it themselves.

MR. DOTY: Let's just take that one step further. What should the teacher do?

JUAN: For one thing, the teacher should bring poetry that relates to the students—ethnically, you know, racially, everything that relates to the students. Otherwise it's like me taking a bird to a school for dogs and telling the dog: "Now fly like that bird." We just can't relate to the poetry of Shakespeare.

JAMES: I would like to elaborate a little on what Juan said. Up at Lincoln University during the summer, we had an Upward Bound program where Juan and myself attacked the administration because of what they were teaching us. I think we shook them up a bit. We didn't accomplish everything that we wanted to, but we started on the road where we wanted to go. I had an English class where they were throwing William Shakespeare and a few others up in my face. I didn't want to relate to it, and I asked if I could teach the English class for at least two days. I was going to show the English teacher how

I thought poetry should be taught. Now, the class was made up of people who weren't really aware of just what poetry was. I thought I would work on this part of their ignorance in my way of presenting poetry. So I got what the students could relate to. I got a few rock 'n' roll records, and I brought them in and played them. They listened to them; they sang to them. Some even got up and danced to them. The next day when I came in, I asked them, "Now just write down something, anything on paper—anything at all." I mean, I didn't confront them with "Don't write those little four-letter words," because this is a limitation. And poetry really has no limitations. I feel teachers limit freedom of expression on paper.

There was a time when teachers were students. I feel that they should often go back to that time when they were sitting at a school desk with pencils in their hands. When they were confronted with William Shakespeare and were asked to write poetry down on the paper, they realized at that moment how hard it is to write poetry.

Today I don't think we are as limited in speech as we used to be. I'm sure, back when most of you went to classes, a word like "damn" or "hell" used in a poem would have caused the poem to be condemned and put aside. "Little Georgie, how could you write such a thing on paper? I will speak to your mother about this."

Today you get away with using "damn," but what about "bitch," "bastard" and words like this? What about those words? These are all part of freedom of speech. If these things have to be written down on paper, they shouldn't be condemned. This is what a person feels, what is within himself. This is what he must bring out; it helps to express what he feels. The hang-up that many students have results from the teacher's refusing freedom of expression.

The teacher will come in and say, "All right, today we'll write poetry."

And a student will say, "Well, I don't know how to write poetry."

"Well, you write poetry or you fail."

That's a threat, and nobody responds to a threat or would like to respond to a threat. And like Juan said, you can't just come in and write poetry. There has to be a time when you want to sit down and write something on paper. Then teachers get into the thing when they ask for a rhyme for a word, like "rare" and "there." You have a heck of a time thinking of another word that will rhyme and make sense. I got into this up at Lincoln University, and I told students that the lines did not have to rhyme—just put down anything. Lines don't have to have any special pattern or any special beat. A lot of teachers like to get into onomatopoeia and this beat and that. Maybe the teacher feels that this is what we ought to be aware of, but I think that these are also limitations to freedom of expression. I think that we should be introduced to poetry gradually. You just can't put a book in front of somebody's face and say, "All right, we're going to read, and we're going to study this book." Then you go on with the same book for a week. The same dull poetry, dull, dull poetry. And then the teacher says, "Copy it. Let me see some of your works of art." But if you put a word like "hell" in there, it's no longer a work of art but a condemnation of art. It's put aside, and the teacher never understands. "Why can't you write poetry?" she says. "Come on, little Georgie, you can write some poetry."

MR. DOTY: Let's get a few questions.

AUDIENCE: Don't you think it would help a student write good poetry if he reads good poetry, even that of another era and another culture?

VERONICA: Could this be like vegetables? My mother says vegetables are good for you. But I don't like turnips. I don't like your poet. How could you make me eat the turnip and listen to your poet? I don't like it. I like other poets. I like other vegetables. Why should I be made to eat that turnip?

AUDIENCE: If you taste turnips and you don't like them, then the hell with turnips. But that doesn't mean that you should take a hang-up attitude toward artichokes. What I don't like is the notion that good contemporary poets are thought to be inhibiting. I don't think they are any more inhibiting of writing than watching Alcindor will keep you from playing basketball. It just seems to me that, in the natural swing of things, you watch the people who are superlative and get ideas.

AUDIENCE: I think what happens a lot of the time is that the teachers are afraid to let go. This is what has to be done first, let go. Let go of the students. Because if you let them go, they'll show you something. Let the students write.

MR. DOTY: Let's start with Veronica West. Her poetry represents a very honest thought and is valuable as an introduction for those who have not enjoyed poetry in the past. Let's have Veronica read two of her poems and then hear from Romani Wardlaw. Then we can all ask some questions.

VERONICA WEST: "Who Am I"

> Who am I?
> If not myself
> Who could I be?
> If not myself
> Who am I?
> Who do I know?
> Where will I go?
> Who will I see?
> If I can't face me.
>
> Love is not by me,
> Fear is beside me,

and with no thought to
        guide me,
Where will I go?
I should ask Alfie,
And then I'd see
what is truly, truly me.

My second poem is: "Light"

Why so dim?
Or is it because you were
made by him?
I don't see why you don't
shine on me,
He lies, cheats, destroys,
yet has the nerve to call me
Boy.
I know my father is a man,
why haven't you shined on him?
You dirty, rotten, stinking
light
Now I know why you're white.

ROMANI WARDLAW: A poem to
        crying faces, dying places,
            the dead gone forever
            Farah, Farah
        People crossing loose and laugh
            See shall they not
            Farah, Farah
        Candid voices loosing threads
            must yell louder
            Farah, Farah
        Paupers giving shallowed livings
            Why push on

Farah, Farah
Stick men winning, growing,
    Sinning? Sin is not
Farah, Farah
nothing from nothing
    Pushing on to nothingness
    Yet we push.   Farah.

"A Mood"

Like wow I'm the only
one here everything
    everybody
is a figment of my
    imagination
I could lay down and
die if I wanted to
    but they
seem so real
    I know
one day I'd wake up
    again
maybe I'll go to sleep
    for a year
sometimes living doesn't
seem worth the bother
I love living but
sometimes I think I'm
going to explode
    boom!
Maybe I'll try that
one day
Maybe one day I'll
    be a fish.

AUDIENCE: May I ask you how you got these kids started?

MR. DOTY: Maybe you better ask them.

AUDIENCE: Did you start in school with your teacher? Did you just sit down and write and write and write and this was what came from it?

ROMANI: I wasn't really inspired at school, because at school they gave me the impression that poetry was words that rhyme.

AUDIENCE: How did you find out different?

ROMANI: One day I was just sitting around and I got into this mean mood, and I just took a look, sort of looking out at the eyes of everybody else. I saw one giant pair of eyeglasses that everybody uses. And I sort of lay on my side and looked. And WOW! You know, I just wrote, and everytime it came on me I wrote again.

MR. DOTY: Her question really is, Romani, how can the teacher in the classroom do anything to push those eyeglasses aside?

ROMANI: You first have to understand the student always.

AUDIENCE: You mean trust the student?

ROMANI: It doesn't have to be trust. You just have to understand. You have to have a learning condition in the class. Most teachers don't have this.

AUDIENCE: What do you call a learning condition?

ROMANI: Learning conditions are where there is no barrier of communication between the teacher and the student. The teacher has to go halfway, and the student has to go halfway, but the teacher has to take the first step. I guess some teachers just weren't meant to be teachers. They think they took the first step, but they just haven't done it. And if you can't make it, neither can the student, and you never have learning conditions. You may stand up there and call yourself a teacher for a year or two years and never get through.

JUAN: Can I make a statement? You can't develop poetry in a student like the students are now. The first thing you have to do is teach. The student has to learn that there is something wrong. The way things are going there is something wrong. Things aren't supposed to be going the way they are going now. Once the student starts to learn, once he starts questioning everything that happens—large and small—once the student says, "Why do you walk with that limp and why doesn't he?", he questions everything. He'll start getting into such a mean psychological thing. For instance, right now I'm projecting my brain. I'm not limited to my mind. Right now my brain is in every one of your heads. It's in every corner of this room, and I'm digging on everything that's happening. And once this student gets into this psychological thing, he will produce.

VERONICA: The problem with teachers is that most of them are statues, molded statues from the same cast. Just like school is a factory which produces statues. You become a secretary or this or that or the other. You're never a piece of artistry, a piece of perfection, but rather that unlimited, unchecked ruin. You're not you, you're still that mold, you're still that cast. You have to break it in yourselves to be artistry. Be a painting; a painting inspires. Be a poem if you want; a poem inspires. Be a tree that one student loves to look at. Be a color that one student loves to see. Be a ball that one child loves to play with. Don't limit yourself. Be anything that you want to be, anything that you think that child will love, will be inspired by. Don't limit yourself. Don't be that statue.

MR. DOTY: One student told me that frequently teachers do take the first step—but it is a step backward and they can't see it as backward. If you feel that this is true, will you give us an example of teachers walking backward?

JAMES: I can give an example of teachers taking backward

steps. There are such things as regulation generals in school systems nowadays. Everything is by the book, which is one step backwards. People who follow the book are products of a system. And if you're a product of a system, how can you produce artists? When you go into a classroom and you pick up a book and say, "We're going to teach poetry," you are expressing yourself as a product of a system.

AUDIENCE: We teachers are responsible for, say, 150 kids a day. Tell us how we can create an environment so that each child can grow to his potential.

JAMES: You're kidding!

AUDIENCE: I'm with you on regulations of the book, but still there are just so many of you to one teacher.

STUDENTS: It's killing me! It's killing me!

ROMANI: You say, how can you create an environment? *You* don't create an environment. Let the students do it. If you create it, that's ten steps backwards. You're starting off wrong already. Students have to do it; you can't create an environment for the students. Don't you see that when you go in there and you try to create an environment for these students, you're putting them in a box and you're going to put everyone in your class in that same box?

AUDIENCE: But in creating an environment, you are also opening up an environment.

ROMANI: But that's the box!

MR. DOTY: What should the teacher do to let the students create this learning environment?

VERONICA: I think that she should open up more. Maybe you do have a hundred or so students, but look at all the days that you have to teach all those students. And in every day that you teach those students, have you really taught anything? Was there a feeling put over? Was any learning process created? I feel that every day every teacher can at least get through to one student. So you have a hundred students, how many days do we have in school? If each day of the year you produced one thought, then you produced a hundred thoughts. You take it day by day. Just don't brainwash them like you people have been doing.

JUAN: I'm talking for myself. I teach a black-literature class at Gratz High School. The students are all black so I relate to black things. I get in the class; I light up my incense and blow it around the room. I get the record player, I turn on a John Coltrane. Okay. I do things that you would never expect to do in a class. I turn the seats around, and I sit on the back with my feet in the chair.

VERONICA [to audience]: Would you do this in class? Isn't that freedom?

AUDIENCE: But we aren't black. How do we approach black students? Let's face it, there are more whites teaching black kids now than there are black teachers for black kids. And white people have to teach black kids.

AUDIENCE: Are we talking about poetry?

JUAN: Yes, we are. If you're teaching poetry, you can't just break it down and say, "It's people." You can't in this country. It's impossible, because ever since this country started it was broken down to a line: black-white, Mayflower-slavery. That was it. And all your life this is the way you are brought up.

AUDIENCE: Are you trying to tell me that Sterling Brown, one of the greatest critics in the United States and a Negro, cannot talk about white literature?

JUAN: He can talk about it, but can he feel it? I mean, you can take a parrot and teach him to say, "Hello, Baby," but that parrot doesn't feel. He's just saying something.

AUDIENCE: The question is not whether a black critic has the ability to read white literature. Nobody's questioning that.

The question is whether black students will be interested in what white people write.

VERONICA: It's the same thing, if I may say so, as a virgin teaching a whore how to do it. Who would know better? Who would be the better teacher—the one with experience or the one without? [*Furor of audience comment and student reply.*]

MR. ROBINSON: Let's come back to the point that an atmosphere has to be built in the classroom if you want a student to understand poetry. We accept the fact that understanding poetry means feeling and that the reason for writing poetry is communicating feeling, thoughts and ideas. The classroom atmosphere must accept all ideas so that students will feel this kind of freedom.

ROMANI [*to a previous questioner in the audience*]: You were asking how you should go about it. As I said, first things first. You have to create a learning situation. The next thing you have to do is break down that authority. You yourself have to be yourself. I mean if you go into the classroom and you feel like putting your feet on the desk, then put your feet on the desk. Don't think, "I can't let the students see me doing this." Be yourself, and tell students to be themselves. Break down that authority.

MR. DOTY: Let me go on with something we were going to bring up a few minutes ago. It is difficult to create an atmosphere of freedom and acceptance in classes of 35 or more students that meet for only 40 or 45 minutes a day—especially when the teacher has to meet as many as 150 students a day. Veronica, for example, would like to sit around and smoke in the classroom. But in my building this is impossible, and I assume it is impossible in yours, too. If this is the situation, maybe we ought to forget it. I'm not sure what the answer is. Maybe we can't teach poetry until we change the schools.

Several of you have mentioned your summer classes at

Ohio Wesleyan. Maybe you would tell us about the atmosphere out there. What was different from the usual classroom?

STUDENT: For one thing it was summertime, and I like the summertime. We could wear shorts to school. We had swimming or tennis instead of regular gym. So most of the time we wore bathing suits. It was very comfortable. We could smoke in class if we wanted to. I think that was because it was a brand-new building. The teachers and students all slept in the same dorm except for the men teachers. It was on a personal basis—teacher, friend also, and student.

VERONICA: It wasn't the master-slave type thing, like Mr. So-and-So, Mr. Doty, Mr. Robinson—where you always have to address them as "Sir."

STUDENT: But teachers had respect from the students. Don't think that because a student calls you by your first name you don't get respect. Teachers are respected or not because of themselves.

We had a class in Integrated Studies in the afternoon. Nobody really wanted to go, because we got up early to have an eight-o'clock class. We were in classes until four. But it was interesting. We broke off into small groups and talked about books. We just didn't read a book and then get tested on it, like *A Tale of Two Cities*. My English teacher at Gratz did that to me.

It seemed like the whole thing was more relaxing. I could really walk out in all the grass and all the trees which I don't find on 30th and Berks. I could just go off and be by myself.

MR. ROBINSON: Okay. That's important. Be by yourself. That may be the learning condition that Romani was talking about.

STUDENT: You have more time to think.

JAMES: I don't know how it is on this campus, but in high

school for ten months out of the year you are confined to the school building. I feel like Romani, who likes to smoke in class. But why confine yourself to a school building? Why not take a trip? Leave the school building, even if it's just to go out in Fairmount Park. That may inspire some type of deep meditation—in getting into your own thing because you can go off on your own and come back at another time.

I want to say something about one of my English classes. Last year in eleventh grade the biggest shock I ever received was when Mr. Robinson came in to teach us after our regular teacher had to leave. I mean he came in with that type of haircut and those glasses. He was—well, I thought he was a big weird-o coming in. I was used to seeing a tie tied properly instead of hanging down. I was used to a very formal atmosphere where everybody was "Mr. This," or "Yes, sir," you know. He was completely different, and it caught me off guard, although I am usually one for being aware, you know. When teachers come in, I am ready to rebel. This teacher came in—Mr. Robinson—and he had rebelled against the system. He had been teaching at another school where he couldn't teach the things he wanted to teach.

MR. ROBINSON: James, let's . . .

JAMES: But this is important, because we were getting some atmosphere in the class. Anyway, we got into a thing where we were very informal with each other, which I feel is very important. The respect will remain there as long as you be yourself. There may be even more respect.

MR. DOTY: The respect remained for you, James. But did it remain for every person in the class?

I want to go on to introduce Juan and ask him to read some of his poetry. I want to introduce him because I am white and he is black. His poetry represents a problem for me and for other white teachers, probably for any teacher. The problem is whether the atmosphere in a classroom is free enough to accept this. Is it free enough to accept the really vulgar images of life? Is the classroom free enough to accept the honest language of students? I think that most teenagers today, when they talk among themselves, use a language which includes four-letter words and images they would be afraid to present to their teacher. I don't know the answer. But as you listen to this, think whether this is acceptable in any classroom. Would you permit it in yours?

JUAN [*lighting incense*]: My first poem I titled "Death."

Be Be Be Bum,
Be Be Be Bum
Be Be Be Be BeBe Be Be Be Bum
    DEATH! DEATH! DEATH!
help, no, please, booo,
no master, spare me jesus.
You whiiiite Deeeviiil,
You whiiiite Deeeviiil,
You white Devil,
You white Devil,
You white Devil,
You white Devil,
Honky Listen!
You dirty animal you,
You living figure of an ultra black shadow.
You existing projection of all artificial everything.
Be Bopping around in your distorted world of fantasy
    DEATH! DEATH! DEATH!
Martha run, oh George, nowhere to run
nowhere to hide, just Doooom,
Took a beautiful world,
and turned it into a playpen of destruction,

all to satisfy your stinking whiiiite bitch!
Do you hear me Napoleon?
Do you hear me Napoleon?
Caesar, Ahaaahaaha,
Hi Ho Silver Awaaaay,
Heil Hitler,
Nixon's the one,
you animal, you beast,
you no good dirty white nigggger.
          DEATH! DEATH! DEAAATH!
Waaa, Momy
wheeeeeee, the whiiite man
Artificial hair, polluted air,
vitamin pills, dollar bills,
drugs made for colds
no deposit no return souls,
but I don't know.
Bing, Bing, Bang, Bang, ungowa
Black Power, Unite, Jumba, uhuru,
Boden Insula,
Sipenda Shetani
ava musalim, woji-woji
Re-vo-lu-tion.
Be Be Be Bum, Be Be Be Bum,
Be Be Be Be Be Be Be Be Be Be Bum,
Vini Vidi Vichi

My next one I wrote after the celebration of Malcolm X's
death—Assassination Day. On the way home I was writing—
walking and writing. This one I wrote from seeing a very
peculiar sight to me. It's titled "An Integration Poem."

Dark, Dark, Dark,
lost, ignorant, confused, coonfused.

C-O-N-F-F-F, Helll.
Roy Wilkins smiling in some white whore's face.
Lou Rawls as Supernigger.
E. Washington Rhodes reading Shakespeare
and quoting John Facenda.
celebrating Lincoln's birthday and the fourth of July.
Negro History Week?
Negro History Week!
Negrooo History Weeek.
I had a dream that one day my boy
and some little white boy will walk along hand in hand,
arm in arm, embracing each other's arms,
with his hand around his waist
and his hand in the crotch of his pants,
and he shall really love that white boy.
Old handkerchief head fool with his thick black lips
rapped around the vagina of some pale, sexless
excuse of a woman,
sucking the bullshit of his existence.
while some poor Sojourner Truth
sits at home with a house full
of snotty nosed, raggedy assed Black Children,
wondering if they will eat tonight.
Some country nigger laying in the gutters drunk
while his Aunt Jemimah wife is scrubbing
Mr. Charlie's drawers.
And what about you Black saleswoman
running around with your corny red wig on,
preaching that big, dumb, ignorant, ugly Black Men ain't shit.
All a Black Man can do for you is to tip you off to a white
    buyer.
Selling, your soul, to the devil.
So he's a Jew, you understand,
but he's got money, more than the Black Man.

Wigs, Make up, Nadanola, Ultra Sheen,
all forms of Artificial Existence,
Professionals of Phonyness!
You have become a friiiied head pet,
a Black Barbie Doll,
a white man's neee-gau.
Rodchester, Steppin Fletchit, High Life,
Buckwheat, come here chile!
Tom, let's go to the cotillion society ball tonight,
ignorant, unaware, hypocritical,
creatures from the white lagoon,
going through changes,
Black! Brown, Yellow! Pink, White!
Mixed colors, mixed blood, dark, lost, ignorant,
confused, cooonfussed, C-O-N-F-F-F.
Integration—A Black chick who thinks she is getting thrills
from a sexless white beast,
Integration—a Black cat who thinks he is getting thrills
from a sexless white Bitch Beast.
Integration—a section in the bus reserved for you,
Integration—a fountain that you can drink from,
Integration—a door you can go through,
Integration—an old tired Black janitor sitting on a toilet stool
next to a white devil.
Integration to sit with the white beast
Integration to shit with the white beast,
Integration to walk like the white beast,
Integration to talk like the white beast,
Integration to act like the white beast,
Integration to look like the white beast,
Integration to almost be a white beast,
Integration perfect world,
integration perfect land,

integration perfect society,
integration perfect America.
My country 'tis of thee
sweet land of slavery,
integration bullshit,
integration—hell,
integration Bulllshittt,
IN-TE-GRA-TION hell!
integration—death.

   Now I would like to read one more. This is more of a round
thing. This is one of the first poems I wrote. It's called "Unite."

Have you ever stopped to notice
if you walk anywhere
You have to make sure
that no hoodlums are there
You'd think that the man
would do his dirt
But it's your own brothers and sisters
Who try to make you hurt.
Your own black brothers trying to beat your head
It makes you feel like dying if you're not already dead.
But here's one thing I can't understand
Why beat on me? Why not beat on the man?
He is the one when there's nothing to do
Except to beat up and kill our brothers, sisters, me and you,
We can't even walk down the streets in peace
Without having to fight these no good police
They rape our women, beat our friends and still
go through the corners and look for our brothers with the
    urge to kill
and then to the corners our black brothers go

as long as this happens the man will control
Now we must learn the black people must unite
Instead of going around always wanting to fight
'Cause as long as he can keep us so very far apart
It pleases him so. It puts joy in his heart.
As long as he sees us black people fight
He feels so content everything's all right
Then he has a chance to do us in
All black is his enemy. All white is his friend.
But if we unite and show him what's in store
And that we won't take this mistreatment any more
And if we unite he will open his eyes
And see we will take no more mess and really be surprised
He'll finally wake up and look all around
He'll pick up instead of putting us down.
But he'll never do this if we constantly fight
He'll just sit back and laugh at this terrible sight.
So if we unite and do all the rest
We'll prove to whitie that black is the best. [*Applause.*]

STUDENT: It's all right to ask questions, isn't it? Well, I knew that everybody might be a little shocked by what Juan read. But I got the feeling that maybe nobody really heard Juan, really heard him when he was reading.

AUDIENCE: What do you mean we didn't hear?

STUDENT: I don't think it really went in.

AUDIENCE: Do you think we would have booed if we had heard it?

STUDENT: No, I don't mean that.

AUDIENCE: This was very moving poetry.

STUDENT: There was no reaction in your faces. That's what I was looking for.

AUDIENCE: We were so intent on his words that we didn't

want to miss a thing. We didn't want to take time to react. What did you expect us to do? Get pale when he said this?

STUDENT: No. I just wanted somebody to look at Juan and say, "Well," or something. You just looked like blank faces that couldn't hear.

AUDIENCE: I don't know what kind of reaction you want.

STUDENT: People just seemed to sit there, and I was curious. Could they really hear?

AUDIENCE: No one smiled. No one murmured. No one said a word. We just sat here intent on every word. Do you remember the reaction to Lincoln's Gettysburg Address? It sounds sacrilegious, but that's the way I felt.

JUAN: We brought this up in the beginning, before I read my poetry. I'd like to know: Is there anyone who would object to me coming in your class tomorrow and reading what I just read?

AUDIENCE: Will you come next week?

MR. ROBINSON: If anyone objects, we'd really like to know why. I think you said you would reject that poem?

AUDIENCE: Yes, I would.

MR. ROBINSON: Why?

AUDIENCE: In the first place, I teach seventh-graders. But regardless of what grade I taught, I would reject it.

MR. ROBINSON: Why? You haven't explained why.

AUDIENCE: You haven't explained some of your reasons, either.

AUDIENCE: I teach retarded seven-year-olds, so I would reject it for my children because they wouldn't understand what it was all about. But I wish my fifth-grade son were here today to hear this.

JUAN: Let me point out one thing. You are a student as long as you are living, because you are always learning. You never finish. Poetry is just an expression of the self. Now, if

I am told, "Curb that. Cross out 'damn,' and 'bitch' and every-thing. Don't say that in front of them." That's castrating me. I'm prostituting myself to you. It's prostituting my feelings, and my feelings are myself. I am castrated right there when I'm not allowed to speak my free mind. You probably know some of the crises of a black youth. But when a black youth is brought up, about the third word he learns is "mother-fucker." Well, this is his life. I was brought up with this, and so it has become a part of my culture. This is part of my lan-guage. That's why I say on some scales the blacks and whites speak two different languages. In a sense they don't com-municate. There's a block.

AUDIENCE: Why can't you learn both languages then? We are learning foreign languages.

MR. DOTY: Instead of just talking about the words, what about the meaning? Probably a much more important term than "motherfucker" is "white devil." These poems are talk-ing about political ideas, about separatism, black identity and so on. The problem of censorship for me, as a teacher, is the problem of political ideas. Certainly that is a much more im-portant problem than the question of language.

AUDIENCE: I'm concerned about that lady who objected to reading that poem to a group of twelve-year-olds. Let me ask you what your reasons are for sloughing off Shakespeare and other good poetry and for failing to expose your children in school to anything that is good. What are your reasons for sloughing it out completely?

VERONICA: I live in a black . . .

AUDIENCE: Let's leave the black part out.

STUDENTS: No! We can't leave . . . I am me. Is this going to erase for a minute . . . This is getting into an argument.

MR. DOTY: Just Veronica.

VERONICA: What I want to say is that I live in a black ghetto around black students, black people, Negroes, and Uncle Toms. And we're in this black school. What other way could I express myself? Who are you as a white person to tell me what is good for me, a black person? What has Shakespeare done for me? Whereas with my black feelings in my poetry I might get across to my people.

AUDIENCE: You said you object to the teachers exposing their children to good literature of the past.

STUDENT: No. She didn't say "exposing." She said "stuffing."

AUDIENCE: Well, I don't like the assumption that we ought to stuff.

ROMANI: Good poetry! Shakespeare's good poetry? Well, maybe I don't feel that way about Shakespeare. As far as I'm concerned, jive Shakespeare.

AUDIENCE: I hate the term "teaching poetry."

ROMANI: You can't *teach* poetry.

AUDIENCE: No. We're not teaching poets. But you can give poetry from the ages. You can give students books to read and read aloud.

ROMANI: You can read it off to them.

AUDIENCE: Do you find that contemporary black poetry helps some students get in the mood to write? A poet like LeRoi Jones?

JUAN: Somebody knows his name!

AUDIENCE: Come on, man, we had LeRoi Jones at our college five years ago. There are some illusions that everybody in the white community is turned off on this stuff. It's not true. I just visited Harlem with a group of Beaver College blacks yesterday. We got to get things in perspective, man.

JUAN: When you say we feel that some whites are just turned off to it, it's because some whites are turned off to it.

JAMES: We're getting into a hang-up. I'd like to comment

on what has been said about stuffing Shakespeare into the curriculum. You know we use Shakespeare as a stereotype to express all the poets that are considered stuffy. We are not establishing the fact that you have to read black poetry to black students in order to get them into the mood. I've read black poetry that confused the hell out of me. I couldn't get into the mood to write by reading that. So we are getting on a black-white basis again, which is always brought up when black and white meet together. I don't care what the subject is, they get on that subject—black and white.

AUDIENCE: I am trying to be objective.

JAMES: But getting objective, you get caught in a hang-up. We are not saying that Shakespeare himself is being stuffed. Poetry is being stuffed into the students. It *is* stuffed. It is stuffed into a student. Do you remember when you were taught poetry?

AUDIENCE: Do you want to know about the so-called great poets?

JAMES: Sure, but don't do it that way.

STUDENT: I am a great poet. Why don't you teach me?

AUDIENCE: Which of the published poets—black, white, old, new—do you enjoy reading? What poetry other than your own?

STUDENTS: LeRoi . . . LeRoi Jones.

JUAN: Let me explain. We're tired. . . . We're up to here with people who write like Shakespeare. Just last month they were pushing a Shakespeare book at me. I forget which one. I'm in twelfth grade now, and he was talking about "ye rose-buds" and "thou shalt fall off the mountain into your backyard" and I'm sitting up here trying to wonder, "What is this man talking about?"

AUDIENCE: In other words, it's because it's strange that it's distant from you?

JUAN: It's alien to me.

AUDIENCE: I think until you can reach the point where you can look to see how someone else's thing is great, you are a captive. You know, I like LeRoi Jones but don't, for God's sake, assume that LeRoi Jones exhausts literature. You know that's hysterical.

STUDENT: I just have a question. It seems like everybody is trying to say what is good and what is bad and what isn't anything. And I want to know who is to say what is good— and what is bad?

AUDIENCE: I want to go back to what was said about white and black. The point is not that Shakespeare is white. The point is that Shakespeare lived in the sixteenth century and wrote in the language of the sixteenth century. If you gave black high-school kids Pushkin and translated it and said, "He was Russian and black and he lived in the eighteenth century," they wouldn't be any more interested in Pushkin's poetry, because it's eighteenth-century poetry. I want to stay away from the hang-up of black and white and don't worry about what one student said about what's good and bad poetry. The only thing you have to go by is what is exciting to the student. If you find that Shakespeare doesn't excite the students, then you have two choices: you either *make* him read Shakespeare, which will guarantee that he will never like it, or try him on something else.

AUDIENCE: Would you be surprised to know that the kids get a bang out of some of these things you're talking about?

AUDIENCE: Some do and some don't.

AUDIENCE: I must say that the communication aspect is a direct and personal thing. Now, Shakespeare never communicates to me very much. Reading is personal, highly personal. Shakespeare doesn't turn me on. This is real. Maybe I'm young; maybe that's why.

MR. ROBINSON: I think it is a safe assumption that most students are turned off by poetry. What can you do to turn kids on to poetry? These kids are turned on to poetry.

AUDIENCE: It's not a question of black, white, green or yellow. It's that some students like this kind of poetry, and some students like that kind of poetry.

ROMANI: There is just one thing. If you're going to present poetry to students, don't put any limitations on it or you're going backwards again.

VERONICA: My statement is a follow-up of hers. In talking about the past, you don't talk about slavery. You don't say those harsh things—how they left the woman on the road and told her that when she finished having her baby, she could catch up. You don't talk about how they cut the baby out of that woman's stomach after they lynched her. So why do you speak of Shakespeare? What is it? If you're not going to bring the facts up from all the way back, from when you started and maybe people had a thought then, a thought or a line that could have been poetry, then why bring up Shakespeare? Who told you that he could be so great? That woman that was lynched was just that important.

JUAN: I would just like to say that the way poetry is taught now is a coverup. Everything is covered up. When you take a child and he says, "How was I born?", you say, "A stork dropped you down the chimney." Everything is covered up. That's what's wrong now. You have to uncover. You got to be real. One of you asked whether I wrote this poetry to shock you. No. It wasn't written for you. It was written for my people. I wrote it to shake them up. To show them what's happening.

MR. DOTY: In conclusion, let me explain that we have talked a good deal about black versus white, black power and so on because that *is* Gratz. That is our school. Juan wrote those poems to communicate with students. Thursday night Juan did a poetry reading for about 300 students in our school auditorium. It's one of the few times I have seen students who came to see a Miss Ebonette Beauty Contest cheer and applaud the reading of poetry. Two of the poems were anti-white. One of them was an accusation to his brothers: "Why do you do this? Why do you fight?" All that I want to say is that Juan communicated.

And in talking about communicating ideas in poetry, I think that what these students have said today emphasizes the importance of the atmosphere in the classroom. Whether you have white students or black students, these students feel that the atmosphere is probably more important than the poetry that is presented.

I think that by "atmosphere" they mean a feeling of freedom, a feeling of acceptance. That includes ideas. It includes language. It includes being willing to expose the things that are important to youth.

Veronica is willing to talk in poetry about the things that are important to her. She wouldn't be willing if the atmosphere were in any way threatening or not free enough. I think that's it.

FLORENCE HOWE and BARBARA DANISH

FLORENCE HOWE, a teacher in Mississippi Freedom
Schools in the summer of 1964, is Assistant Professor
of English at Goucher College and a member of the
Board of Teachers and Writers Collaborative.
BARBARA DANISH, a junior at Goucher College, is a
poet, artist and choreographer.

Experiment in the Inner City

FLORENCE HOWE: A recent report of the Washington school system describes "the main problems of the English department at the secondary level . . . as centering around 'curriculum, lack of suitable materials, lack of communication, low morale, and poor teachers.' That is, they center around everything." It is, no doubt, impossible to change "everything," at least at once. And Washington's may be an extreme case. But it is probably safe to assume that several aspects of English at the secondary level might be improved.

High-school English teachers are unquestionably overworked and underhelped. The large numbers of students that such teachers are responsible for gives them, if they are diligent, a heavy load of paper-grading each evening. No matter how diligent teachers may be, their schedule usually makes it totally impossible for them to give students the individual attention they may need; nor are teachers usually able—either through preference or training—to work with students in small groups.

Thus, the English classroom all too often is, as many have described it and as I have observed it, a room in which the only voice heard is the teacher's. The students sit in rows, silently listening or tuned out, or on occasion awaking to answer a specific question. All too often the purposes of an English classroom—communication, talking, listening, responding to each other, thinking, writing and reading to and for each other—are lost.

Two of the problems have to do with the ratio of students to teachers and the style of teaching that prevails. A third problem related to both of these is the curriculum. Most high-school teachers of English have been trained in literature and language written before 1900 and often British rather than American; and most standard high-school curricula still consist not only of works written primarily before 1900, but of surveys of British literature from Beowulf through the nineteenth century. Some of this is just beginning to change, but until recently, most high-school teachers I worked with had never read a poem written by even now dead twentieth-century poets such as William Carlos Williams and e. e. cummings, much less by LeRoi Jones, Gregory Corso, David Henderson or Henry Braun. They have never tried to write poems in their own language and rhythms. How, then, can they teach their students to write freely and creatively or to enjoy and understand literature?

I have spent most of the past twenty years teaching undergraduates, the last nine at Goucher College, where I devote a major portion of my time to twentieth-century poetry. Ever since the summer of 1964, when I went to Mississippi to teach in a Freedom School, I have also been experimenting with my own teaching. For I discovered then that my own classroom was not very different from the high-school one I have just described; my voice filled the hour. I used to lecture and march, before rows of faces, stopping occasionally for a question-and-answer debate with a single student; but I never considered the possibility of engaging students in discussion with each other.

My experimenting in 1964 took the form, first, of arranging chairs in a circle rather than in rows. By sitting down in a circle, I deliberately changed my relationship to my students. They were not all looking at me anymore; they could now see each other as well. Sitting down, I don't mind confessing, tended to shut me up, to help me to listen to students. If I was silent, moreover, then someone else had to speak. Lectures gave way to group discussion, and I began to become a resource for the group. In the course of five years, I have experimented with many varieties of what can be called a "student-centered" or "nonauthoritarian" teaching style. For the sake of this paper, I want to describe the way in which my poetry classes work.

I teach a course called "Introduction to Poetry," usually elected by sophomores. For the course I order several anthologies and four or five volumes of poems by contemporary poets, often those who will be visiting Goucher that year. On opening day I work out an arrangement whereby groups of students take alternating responsibility for choosing the specific poems to be discussed from day to day. For an early discussion last year, students chose a poem called "The Language" by Robert Creeley:

THE LANGUAGE

Locate *I*
love you some-
where in

teeth and
eyes, bite
it but

take care not
to hurt, you
want so

much so
little. Words
say everything,

I
love you
again,

then what
is emptiness
for. To

fill, fill.
I heard words
and words full

of holes
aching. Speech
is a mouth.[1]

We were thirty in a room so small that we could achieve a
circle only by lining the four walls with our chairs. This is
the way the class began:

ME: Does anyone want to read the poem?
SUSIE [*reads the poem fluently, as though it were a prose sen-
tence. Silence.*]

ME: Does anyone else want to read the poem? [*I had already established, in an earlier class, that this was standard procedure. We would have as many readings as there were volunteers.*]

JUDY [*reads, paying close attention to the line breaks and stanza form. Silence again, this time accompanied by shocked faces.*]

ME: Judy, why did you read it that way?

JUDY: Because I heard Creeley read once last year, and that's how he did it. [*Silence, and more shocked faces.*]

There followed a discussion across the room, with me acting as chairman, about whether the halting version made sense or added anything to the poem. When the discussion had seemingly been stalled by a student who said that reading styles were just a matter of taste, I asked, "What feeling is the poem after? How does the poem make you feel when it's read in the second, halting way?"

We had another reading of it, and the students were then quick to respond that the speaker in the poem sounded "unfluent," as though he were struggling for words, hesitant, unsure of himself. Moreover, it turned out that those students who wanted the poem read smoothly—"so that it made sense," they said—saw the poem empty of hesitation or struggle, simply as a definition of language. If anything, it seemed an accident to them that it was a poem at all.

The hour ended without my saying that one group was right, the other wrong, though there was pressure for me to do just that. My response to the pressure was that there was plenty of time for them to work this out for themselves since we would be reading dozens, perhaps hundreds of poems. They could keep this question in mind. And it did not take them long to discover, in the course of similar hours, that many contemporary poets, like Creeley, write poems that *emit feelings* through their form, as much as through words and images. Hence, it is important to pay attention to the way the poem is lined on a page. But I won't belabor the point further.

I believe that students learn when classrooms become places for discovery. Poetry, moreover, is particularly responsive to this teaching style, since no amount of lecturing about the so-called meaning of one poem will teach anyone anything about another poem. Poems, particularly in their twentieth-century versions, tend to be discrete, unique worlds. Ways into one poem will not lead necessarily into another.

During the same years that I was learning to teach in a way new to me, I was also aware that undergraduates were striking out into teaching. In 1964, for example, about 700 college students staffed Mississippi's Freedom Schools. Since then, thousands more have taught in tutorial programs as well as in the hundred or so free universities and experimental colleges they have organized all over the country. Upward Bound's 300 or more projects have successfully used college students as tutor-counselors, staff members paid not only to provide a model for the high-school students' emulation, but also to reach the high-school student as the teacher often cannot. Two years ago I began to think about a means of using the potential energy and ability of college students that equip many of them for the kind of innovative and flexible teaching needed especially in urban schools today.

In customary fashion, I began by experimenting with my own students at Goucher. I started dividing my poetry classes into small groups, asking that students take turns being chairman and recorder. Recorders were to turn the discussion into group papers that would, in turn, feed back into class discussion. At first, we used class time, with the four groups in the four corners of the room, and with me wandering among them, trying to find a role for myself in the process. What came out of it was a sense that half or more of the students found the small groups energizing. They liked my absence, and some of them were willing to admit this. They were free to discuss among themselves matters that they thought I might find peculiar or silly or ignorant. But the most important discovery substantiated my original guess: students reported that they learned a great deal, especially from leading the group or being responsible as active participants. In other words, they *learned from teaching,* at least as I had begun to define teaching.

The idea is one that now seems self-evident. All good teachers know that they learned to teach by teaching and, equally important, most teachers report that they learned more about their subject matter is one year of teaching than they had in years of study in college. Psychologists and other social scientists have also been extolling the virtues of active participation. In fact, there are some signs that educators have heard them. A good deal of elementary-school curriculum is now organized around the notion of learning through discovery; and some Master of Arts in Teaching programs attempt to combine teaching and course work. But, by and large, high schools and colleges have not been quick to seize on this idea.

My original proposal, written in the fall of 1968, asked Goucher College and the Baltimore City Public Schools to join with the Teachers and Writers Collaborative, which was funding me, to try an experiment in which undergraduates would teach poetry to small groups of high-school students twice a week for a period of ten weeks. To get the project going required a number of meetings with officials of both Goucher College and the Baltimore City Public Schools. Last year we agreed that the project would have extracurricular status at Goucher, although it was granted official status in the

Baltimore schools. That is, the undergraduates and I added the project to our normal spring programs. In March of this year we became an experimental course at Goucher.

For the high-school students, these poetry hours replace two of their regular English classes. Last year we were placed in Mergenthaler Vocational-Technical High School. Our 63 tenth-graders were boys, all but 12 of them white. A few wanted to become teachers, most were going to be auto mechanics or were studying industrial electronics. As one might expect, they were at first delighted by the idea of being taught by pretty Goucher girls, but rather put off by poetry. The procedure in each of the 11 groups was similar. We used mimeographed sheets of poems in lieu of textbooks. Last year the undergraduates were responsible for choosing their own poems, subject to approval by the teachers and supervisors. They had only one restriction from me: that they were to offer their students a real choice of poems. We wanted to discover what poems high-school students really wanted to discuss. After each teaching session, the undergraduate wrote her journal describing the experience. The following is a journal account of opening day:

April 25: Today was the first day. I took my group into the TV room and asked them to make a circle. I introduced myself as Miss Bass and asked them if they would tell me what they would like to be called. They said Reggie, Wes, Scott, and Bob. One boy was absent, Gil. Then, without any other preliminaries I passed out a sheet of four poems and asked them to look them over and see if any were familiar (since two were popular songs) or if they liked any. Reggie was a little confused as to whether the sheet was all one poem or what, and I explained that there were four poems. Okay. Bob suggested "Dock of

the Bay" and I asked whether he'd read it. He smiled and
did.   —ELLEN BASS

In their own journals the high-school students also com-
mented on the project. Although a number expressed enthu-
siasm for the experiment, some were more cautious. ("The
poetry class yesterday was not as much of a bore as I thought
it would be.") A couple declared that it had been something
of a "drag." Several students were quick to note and appreciate
two fundamental assumptions of the experiment. The first was
simply that the undergraduates' knowledge of and enthusiasm
for poetry would rub off or spill over onto the high-school stu-
dents. One boy, in effect, described this process:

> You can get a lot of meanings out of a poem. Actually
> it all depends on the way you read them. The student
> teacher seemed to like poetry pretty much. She also had
> a good sense of humor. I think that I could learn to like
> poetry if I read it steadily.   —WESLEY LLOYD

The second assumption was that the discovery method of
instruction was more effective than lecturing. The high-school
students described aspects of this method, occasionally with
wonder and pleasure as well as bewilderment. For example:

> But the way they teach is a little off. Like our first les-
> son, most of us don't know the first thing about poetry
> except that some rhyme and some don't. What I mean is
> that when you have your first introduction they should
> like give meanings and describe and explain poetry and
> its different or various types. Maybe they'll get around to
> it sometime during the process or I'll start asking ques-
> tions.   —REGINALD JOHNSON

All of the boys' early comments suggest that while there was some questioning of the novel methods being used, the high-school students were flexible enough to adapt to these readily. For the most part, they enjoyed the new freedoms and responsibilities offered them. Even more significant is that they trusted the undergraduates almost at once: their rapport was as good as I had expected it to be. Partly this was, of course, a factor of age. It was easier to talk to near-contemporaries about serious subjects that matter than to trust someone older, more teacherly, and hence suspect. From the beginning, the undergraduates were able to focus discussion on poems and subjects of seriousness: death, war, race, and glue-sniffing were favorites in spite of, or because of, their gloom.

Barbara Danish, an undergraduate who taught in the project, can tell you better than I about her experience.

BARBABA DANISH: I never wanted to be a teacher. My one constant promise to myself was that once I was out of school, I would never go back. For any reason. When people asked me what I was going to be when I grew up, and suggested I might be a teacher, I said, "No, I will never be a teacher."

When I was a first-term sophomore, and I am now a junior, I had a course with Florence called "Introduction to Poetry." Our first assignment was to write what our goals were in this course. I wrote that I was not so interested in how to read or analyze poetry, as I was in the writing of poetry. My goal was respected, and I wrote for the whole term. In writing poetry I learned its constructions. This was the first time I had had a teacher who let the student decide what she wanted out of the course, who let the student work with her own goals and grade herself accordingly. If a class could be like this, if a teacher could do this, I thought, perhaps school could be good. Perhaps it could be helpful for the student and flexible to her needs and desires.

From September of that year until April, when we started teaching in the project, I had two poetry courses and attended a poetry workshop where we usually discussed our own poetry. All of this time, I was writing. I wasn't paying much attention to class or to what the rest of the class was doing. And maybe this is in itself the open question of the whole thing. Because on my first day of teaching at Mergenthaler, I found myself asking questions the way Florence had asked them, questions about how someone felt about the poem, and I found myself getting a sincere and enthusiastic response. You understand that while I thought I had been learning about writing poetry, I had also been getting an understanding of poetry and an approach to studying poetry—an approach which could get people easily into a poem.

We call such an approach using open questions as opposed to closed questions.* In closed questions, either the answer is in the question or the question is mechanical and the answer can be found, almost paraphrased, in the piece of literature. For example, let's look at a poem by Gregory Corso:

LAST NIGHT I DROVE A CAR

Last night I drove a car
    not knowing how to drive
    not owning a car
I drove and knocked down
    people I loved
    . . . went 120 through one town.

---

* Florence Howe and Paul Lauter began to use the terms "open" and "closed" questions as a result of their experimental teaching in the Mississippi Freedom Schools in 1964 and at an N.D.E.A. Institute at Goucher College in 1965. See also the explanation at the end of this chapter.

> I stopped at Hedgeville
> and slept in the back seat
> . . . excited about my new life.[2]

If I were to have a closed-question discussion about this poem, it might go something like this:

TEACHER: What is the boy in the poem doing?
STUDENT: He's driving a car.
TEACHER: But he says he doesn't know how to drive a car.
STUDENT: [*Silence.*]
TEACHER: Whom did he knock down?
STUDENT: People he loved.
TEACHER: Why did he knock them down?
STUDENT: He was driving too fast.
TEACHER: Is it nice to knock people down?
STUDENT: No.

Through closed questions I have given the students no opportunity to express any way they might feel about the poem. I have told them this is a poem, which they might have otherwise questioned; I have told them it is a boy speaking. How do I know? I have also tried to make a moral out of the poem, and I have directed all the questions so that I will finally make the student say, "Yes, he was bad for driving when he didn't know how and for stealing a car."

Of course, it needn't be a moral I'm trying to get at. In one discussion we heard in a Baltimore high school about an essay on Helen Keller, the teacher asked what the author thought of Helen Keller. Students gave many answers, but the teacher didn't respond to any of them until someone said, "He thinks she's courageous," and then she said, "Yes, courageous." The teacher was waiting for the answer she wanted. In open questions we don't wait for any specific answers, and nothing is flatly right or wrong.

Something you may have noticed in the dialogue was that there was rarely a connection between the questions asked. Each was an isolated question, not a logical follow-up to the question that had gone before or, more important, to the answer that had gone before. I would like to read a part of my journal about discussing the same poem in open-question fashion.

I gave them the sheet and said to choose one. They chose "Last Night I Drove a Car." Leroy said, "This Corso—he's a weird guy—he gets all excited about knocking people down." I asked if he was knocking people down. He said, "Well, yeah, it says, 'I drove and knocked down people I loved'—he hit 120." I said, "It says he went 120. Is he really knocking people down?"

LON: It says he went 120 through one town.

LEROY: No, it talks about people he loved—knocking them down—and then it says he got 120 in one town. I said, "Did he really knock people down?"

LON: No, he took this car, so he made his mother and father and relatives who love him feel bad.

MIKE: Look then, why did he say "knocked down"? He killed them.

LON: Why would he want to kill people he loved?

MIKE: Then why did he say "knocked down"? Why didn't he make it so people could understand?

LEROY: Yeah, you said he stole the car because he said "not owning a car." Why didn't he say "steal"?

Lon said he liked it. "It sounds destructive. That's why he did it. He's real psyched up. It's real cool."

I asked if he would ever do it again.

They said, "Sure, man. He'll do it he's caught."

LEROY: Yeah, it's legal till you're caught.
We discussed whether taking your father's car was stealing.

Of course, when I was in high school, if the teacher ever asked an open question like "What do you think of this?", we figured she was stalling for time until the period was over, or she didn't have anything else to ask, so we didn't even bother to answer it. Anyway, if anyone answered, it was more likely to get laughed at or frowned at than accepted as an opinion. For example, if a closed-question teacher asked me what I thought about "Last Night I Drove a Car," and I answered, "I like it. It sounds destructive," I'd probably get a lesson on how I should be respectful of other people's property. I wouldn't ever offer an honest feeling again. I would give the teacher the answer I knew she wanted. Obviously, if an open question is to be asked, and the teacher wants an honest response, there has to be more than an occasional, isolated question. The class itself has to be an open place where students have a choice in what they study, and where discussion is based on open questions.

The use of open questions doesn't mean the teacher has no place in the classroom. She is still a leader, usually more proficient in reading poetry, asking questions and therefore directing discussion than her students. Every clue that a student gives while he is reading, while someone else is reading or during the discussion—can be used to get into the poem. At first, not being skilled with handling open questions and picking up clues, I was not able to get far into the poem, and I missed a lot of chances for discussion. As both the students and I became more experienced in talking about poetry, talking with each other, and following questions and answers, we were able to get more deeply into the poem.

The students had a choice about the poems we would discuss. Twice during the project I gave them page-long poems, but usually I gave them a page of short poems to pick from. At first I would ask, "Well, which one do you want to read?" When someone suggested a poem, I would ask who wanted to read it, and we would proceed from there. Later someone would just start reading a poem that interested him. Of course, once in a while there was no poem they wanted to read, but an open question deals with this by asking, "Why don't you like any of these?" It's important to work with negative as well as affirmative response to the poetry. For example, on the first day, we had a sheet with four poems: "Pop Poem" by Ronald Gross, which they hardly looked at, a long poem which they hardly looked at because of its length, "The Eagle" by Tennyson, which they looked at and discussed for a minute, and "Jimmie's Got a Goil" by e. e. cummings. My journal reads:

> I asked if they liked the poem. They didn't. They had trouble reading it, especially "coitnly." They laughed. It wasn't well read. No one else wanted to read it. They said, "There's something wrong with it. Things are spelled wrong. Whoever wrote it is a foreigner or wants to sound cute. He doesn't know how to spell." They said it wasn't a poem. I asked why and they said because it didn't say anything. I asked why he wrote it. They said, "Well everybody envies someone for something and this guy envies another guy for his girl. He wants her because she can shimmie and twist and twirl."

From the beginning we hadn't used traditional school poems. Most of the poems were like "Last Night I Drove a Car." They weren't about subjects that poetry was supposed to be about. One day we were reading one of Henry Braun's poems, "The Wrestlers," because he was to visit us the next day.

Mike read "The Wrestlers."

LON: You can't write poems about wrestlers. Poems are about beautiful things like love. [*Snicker*.]

MIKE: They don't have to be.

LON: Well, I thought poems were just about intangible things.

ME: What about "Airplane Glue"?

LON: Well, that's different.

ME: And where the boy cut his hand off with a saw?

LON: Yeah, well that's different, too.

ME: And "Last Night I Drove a Car"?

LON: Well, maybe I don't know what I'm talking about.

MIKE: You can write about anything, like that chair over there. About the metal and where it came from and everything.

LON: Well, write it.

MIKE: Naw, I can't.

LON: You can so. [*To me*.] He's really intelligent.

ME: Well, why don't you try?

LON: I'll write about dirt.

They start writing. Showing each other. Crossing out. Asked if they were writing a poem.

This was our first day of writing. Often after that we would get into writing because it helped solve a problem we were having with a poem we were reading. For instance, perhaps you noticed that one boy in my group translated everything quite literally while another one could interpret things on a more abstract level. Most of the times we could still communicate, but sometimes discussion was difficult. For example, one day we were talking about "Complete Destruction" by William Carlos Williams:

> It was an icy day.
> We buried the cat,
> then took her box
> and set match to it.
>
> In the back yard.
> Those fleas that escaped
> earth and fire
> died by the cold.[3]

MIKE: Yeah, I think I get it. The cat died and when the fleas crawled out of the fire, it was so cold that they died, too.

LON: It must have some other meaning. I don't think he meant cat. I think he's trying to put some point across, but I don't know what it is.

MIKE: Well, if he says "cat," he should mean cat.

We had written before, so I suggested that maybe there was more than a cat and his fleas dying, and perhaps we could try writing a poem which said one thing on the surface and could also be interpreted on another level. In other words, why didn't we write a poem where we consciously made the non-literal translation what we meant? Mike, the literalist, wrote:

> Many men work to support and comfort others.
> For all I know they may have injured themselves
>   Take a good look at the sweat
> Put into it the craftsmanship and maybe sore
> muscles in this
>   All this takes place while people sit around.

Lon wrote:

THE MAN

The Man who
Died flew high
in the sky
never to be
seen.

But yet-in-the-high
mountains
he is still heard
as he is perched
on his roost.

With Mike's poem we got into a discussion of lining and how to emphasize things when you're writing a poem. While Mike continued to interpret poems literally, I think that at least while he was reading the poem, he understood the concept of an image, and that a poet can mean more things than a cat. However, while he admitted in later discussions that there were such things as images, he still did not understand why the poet didn't just say what he meant.

With Lon's we talked about the subject of the poem. I asked why he had written it and he said, "It was just an inspiration, a miracle." Then we asked him to explain it. He didn't have to. One of the rules of writing was that you never had to show it to anyone or answer any questions about it. But he answered, "Well, if a man dies, you say a man dies, and if a bird dies, you say a bird dies. But if a great bird is extinct, then it's like a man. That is just the way I see it."

The guys liked writing. At the beginning of the project they had said once about a cummings poem, "If we had written that, the teacher would throw it away, but just because this guy cummings wrote it, it's a poem." Well, in the project their poems were treated like cummings'. And it was thrilling for them to see their poems mimeographed and discussed seriously. The first week they were all going to be poets. They all offered their autographs. By the end of the project they agreed that poets probably don't write just for money, as they had thought at the beginning.

My thoughts and abilities also changed during the project. As a teacher, I developed skill in asking questions, steering a discussion, getting into a poem. I have hardly mastered the technique and obviously need more work in getting into abstract questions such as, "If he means cat, why doesn't he say it?" As a poet, I found that the project erased any lingering thoughts I might have had that one has to be in a certain mood to write. I wrote when everyone else did. Even more than before the project, I was learning to understand different styles of writing by being conscious of how I wrote poems, and why I lined in particular ways, or used certain punctuation or certain words. And I could use this knowledge in the discussion, particularly discussion about the kids' own poems.

I would like to read a poem I wrote while the project was going on about the teaching, the boys, their personalities and their environment.

> *To Leroy Caswell, Michael Fiorenza,*
> *Mike O'Conner, Ronnie Onheiser,*
> *Doug Sentz and Lonnie Splain, poets.*
> *Read this. Your words have decided a life.*

    you are precious to me
    i have never said: I am a poet

I

down harbored streets
  i walked where The Words come in

coming in so fast
one cannot hold each one
as he might have done before he knew them
but he must hammer them
break and build them
perhaps even spit on them
to make them new
for the old person

yes.
in the course of an afternoon
when one is faced with so many buckets of words
  (and what is the use of The Words at all)
one wonders exactly
what to do with them
one cannot save them
but who would want to anyway
one can only use them
  (we sat in a circle
  so the words could catch in the middle
  and go each way, toward each of us)

II

mine were six
i knew them
from time to time
  now and again from their smiles
  when they let a real one out

or from the arm on the back of their chair
or the bored paper folded in their hand,
from their faces.

(If I walked alone
along Highland Town streets

(If I wandered to
a darkened door and met six bright blades

Once a man (a boy if you like)
walking the streets
was felled by a telephone pole:
with it across him
he could not move

one night there was
a dance
five knives battled
and twenty fists
and at the end
one policeman
lay in dazed blood
on the hall floor

a nickel
or a nickel bag
   here
   where no step
   is too big
   or too slow
   or too too grand
      what you have said

is the truth, poets
and more truth
than i have known before
you have decided my life with your truths

time and again
i have sucked deeply in
different worlds
and rejoiced in them
that killed me after

the truths were thrown out
when he laughed
his laughs evaded truth
and mocked himself

six black birds
put into a single pie
of rotted fruit
flew out
in splendid finery
and asked for an amnesty
granted
and ate sweet peaches and grapes

Poets, will you leave your heads open
And let the words keep singing in?

FLORENCE HOWE: I want to talk about two more matters.
What did people learn from this experiment? What is its pos-
sible usefulness? And second, why poetry? Why do we spend
all this energy on reading and writing poems anyway? Why
do we think it's important for the high-school curriculum?

Barbara has told you about the usefulness of the experiment for her as a poet and a teacher. Other undergraduates would write a somewhat different account of their experience—several of them have done so—but the general message is plain enough. The project deepened their ability to understand poetry and initiated them positively into teaching. Actually, we had all expected that the experience would be a good one, and we were not disappointed.

More exciting for all of us, however, was the discovery that the undergraduates had, indeed, taught something particular to the high-school students. We decided, late in the experiment, that we would give the high-school students four poems to write about, in a nonthreatening arrangement, supervised by the undergraduates themselves. The results were extraordinary. In 13 sessions high-school students had learned how to approach a poem fearlessly. (That's especially good when you consider how many of us have sat through 40 or 45 hour-long courses only to discover that we could not write about a poem or a story without first going to the library to see what the critics think of it.)

The high-school students wrote easily and well on poems that they had never seen before. Especially interesting was their use of affective language: they "liked" the poem they chose because it made them "feel" sad or happy or sorry for something. They knew how to get into a poem independently, either through finding out how it made them feel or by finding an analogous experience in their own lives to what was going on in the poem. Cummings' balloon man, for example, reminded one of the boys of how he used to run after the popsicle man when he was little.

If we learned that we could teach high-school students effectively, we also learned that we had not affected their teachers. That people learn from doing was brought home to me more sharply than ever, since we had failed to provide any role other than that of observer for the two teachers. But we have learned from our error. This year's four teachers will, like the undergraduates, teach small groups and write journals about their experience.

This brings me to the question of the experiment's value for the high-school teacher generally. So long as class size remains at 35 to 40, it will be difficult to implement the open class discussion I advocate. But it is possible to teach high-school students to run their own group discussions. Certainly, it would also be possible for high-school teachers and a nearby college to work out an arrangement similar to the one I have been describing. Apart from these matters, the most obvious value of the project has seemed to school people, from the first, the accumulation of a body of tested poems and ideas for their use in the classroom. Clearly, the rapport between undergraduates and high-school students allows us to expect a special kind of honesty about choices here. Last year the undergraduates functioned autonomously, each choosing those poems she felt comfortable with or thought her group would enjoy. The duplication we felt we achieved was either accidental or the result of reported success; occasionally, there was deliberate sharing of curriculum. This year, however, we agreed to collect curriculum in advance and to follow, with some allowance for flexibility, an arranged order of poems. About half of these are ones used last year, the rest new. Together they will make a good anthology of poems for high-school students.

But why spend all this energy on poetry? Why should poems seem a panacea for the English classroom? There are at least three obvious advantages. First, poems are brief enough to allow their form to be easily perceived and to permit reading to be independent of "homework" or preparation. Like a small artifact, a poem can be held in the hand and the eyes. It's all there to talk about, point to for evidence and clues, and read aloud. In this sense, it's a particular joy and pleasure that more bulky pieces of literature are not.

Here's a little poem, "Spring and All," by William Carlos Williams:

> so much depends
> upon
>
> a red wheel
> barrow
>
> glazed with rain
> water
>
> beside the white
> chickens[4]

A poem's precise and expressive use of language promotes a functional approach to the study of language: a poem demands that you talk about words, possibly grammar and punctuation as well. And you can always ask, Why? Why the red wheelbarrow? Why the parentheses in a cummings poem? Why no punctuation at all in some poems? Why all those commas in a funny poem by William Jay Smith that we use in early sessions?

POET

After, each, word, he, places, a, comma,
A, remarkable, insight, indeed,
It, gives, you, jitters, when, you, look,
It, gives, you, hiccoughs, when, you, read.[5]

Needless to say, recent American poems are written in language accessible to the student, needing no translation, and rich in contemporary connotation.

Third, the poem's expression of contemporary thought and feeling should stir responses from the students, thus making discussion possible. Contemporary poetry, unlike most of the poetry of the past, is relevant to our lives and those of our students. Poets are writing about questions of war and peace, about violence, insanity, drug addiction and so on. This is most obvious, and yet we will have to work very hard here to encourage school people and to educate parents. If we are timid about introducing certain subjects into the curriculum—sex and love, for example—we must also be aware that poets have written more fully and perhaps more sanely on this subject than most. And we must understand that no other subject is more keenly in the minds and feelings of adolescents and more absent from the school curriculum.

There are at least three other values inherent in the use of poetry, not so immediately apparent as those I mentioned above. First, the uniqueness and inventiveness of twentieth-century poetic forms provide models for writing: the ideal is individual invention, but the forms are often tight. For example, here is an apparently simple poem by William Carlos Williams:

THIS IS JUST TO SAY

I have eaten
the plums
that were in
the icebox

and which
you were probably

saving
for breakfast

Forgive me
they were delicious
so sweet
and so cold[6]

After discussing this poem and arguing about whether it was a poem or a note, a pair of high-school students in one group wrote the following imitation.

This is just to say
that I used
the drill press
without permission

And I broke
the chuck

I'm sorry
but it was
a lot of
fun.
—JOE and RICHARD

Later Richard invented his own form for a poem about drugs:

Drugs!
liquids
solids
gases

Excell in zooming minds to unknown worlds!
Like miniature spaceships in disguise!
a trip,
    a return, and
Eternal doom for some people upstairs.
                                —RICHARD D. JOHNSON

Trying to invent their own forms, aiming at succinct, precise expression, students learn to use language freely within restrictions they are responsible for controlling and maintaining. Writing poetry is as useful for developing what we call "language skills" as writing essays. And often lots more fun.

The second value is the most intangible and yet probably the most important of all, since it has to do with the nature of poetry and the nature of man. Poetry is, as Wordsworth has said, "feeling intellect." That is, a poem is an expression of feeling and thought caught in a form as symbolic as language itself. The statement is abstract—as all statements about poetry tend to be—but the poem is never abstract. The study of any single poem is the study of the connection between feeling and thought, a connection made explicit by the poem's rhythm and pattern. The discussion of a poem, the working out in detail of a poet's thought and feeling, may help students not merely to grow more articulate about their own thoughts and feelings, but to become increasingly conscious of the connection between feelings and thoughts, and so to promote clarity of judgment and vision. I could use any number of undergraduate diaries to report on how this may happen, but since relations between the races have rarely been worse, let me illustrate from a discussion in one of the few integrated groups we had last year.

Debbie's students had avoided all poems about race; but once, in a discussion of a poem on drugs, a white boy had excitedly used the word "nigger." Debbie reported that once he had heard himself, he and the other white boy present "giggled hysterically." Her journal continued:

> The black guys ignored it. I did too. Maybe I shouldn't have—was very tense—didn't want to play Champion of Civil Rights—we went on—so it dropped unmentioned, not unnoticed, I'm sure; but I'm sure this isn't the first time—.

A week later Debbie brought in a sheet containing Kenneth Patchen's poem "Nice Day for a Lynching":

> The bloodhounds look like sad old judges
> In a strange court. They point their noses
> At the Negro jerking in the tight noose:
> His feet spread crow-like above these
> Honorable men who laugh as he chokes.
>
> I don't know this black man.
> I don't know these white men.
>
> But I know that one of my hands
> Is black, and one is white. I know that
> One part of me is being strangled,
> While another part horribly laughs.
>
> Until it changes,
> I shall be forever killing; and be killed.[7]

Here is part of Debbie's account of the hour:

> June 11. . . . "The Lynching" by Kenneth Patchen. They chose "The Lynching" immediately, saying that

they thought it was really good. . . . Why? "Tells it like it is." . . . Richard interjected that we better not discuss this poem 'cause it'll bring out everybody's prejudice. ME: "Don't you think prejudice is an important thing to talk about?" No responses. . . . I asked who the speaker was, and the general consensus was that it was a white man. I asked if it made a difference in the poem whether the speaker were white or black. The boys argued that it had to be a white man, because a black man wouldn't be standing in the crowd watching another black man get lynched, because if a crowd was that angry, they'd get him, too. Some discussion of the time of the poem followed. Emerson had to instruct the others that lynching still occurred in the South. . . .

At this point a really interesting thing happened. A Negro girl who was in the room washing the blackboards raised her hand. Joe called my attention to her. I asked her if she wanted to sit down and discuss the poem with us. She did, and she began to analyze the poem aloud completely. . . . It was the first time in the year that someone had given an "analytic monologue" on a poem. The guys were fascinated with her ability and relieved, I think, that they didn't have to express themselves on the subject. The girl said "all the right things" about the poem—in terms of white guilt and prejudice and the necessity for bettering race relations. "Well, I guess that takes care of it," Joe said. . . . The guys understood. They wanted to drop it. I wouldn't let them. "Do you agree with the poet?" General agreement. "It's a big ideal," Richard said. "That's the way everybody should feel, but they don't." General agreement. "Why do you think the poet wrote the poem?"

—to say you shouldn't lynch people

> —because he saw this guy getting lynched and he got
> sick
> —because he was down South and saw conditions there
> and wanted to write against them
>
> —DEBORAH STONE

The bell ended the hour and Debbie ends her entry with a wry comment: "No super-breakthrough in communication, but at least I threw the subject at them." No comment is probably necessary about the maturity with which the undergraduates were usually able to handle sensitive matters like race and drugs. But it was on the question of maturity, I might add, that school people were, to begin with, most suspicious about the undergraduates. Needless to say, we will have to keep convincing them.

Finally, the third value, Wordsworthian as well. It has to do with the love of literature preceding, *and* motivating, the study of literature. The relationship between skill-training and motivation is often debated by teachers of English. I feel certain that motivation—the deep-rooted variety—must precede any meaningful learning, even of skills. Students who get interested in books, reading, ideas, learn everything with greater ease. Moreover, students who read a great deal do, simply through that process, enlarge their vocabularies, straighten their syntax, improve their grammar. Students who are curious and eager to learn are receptive even to correction. They will engage in skill-training with some sense of its usefulness, moreover, if they begin not blindly, but with some vision of the power of language and idea. It has been my experience with both high-school and college students that twentieth-century poetry provides that vision. Hence, I would argue that poetry is *interesting,* naturally appealing, relevant.

To illustrate, I want to report on a workshop with the undergraduates on John Holt's *How Children Fail.* Discussion had moved from the role of the teacher to Holt's view of curriculum, particularly to his argument that there is no longer a body of knowledge that one can insist that students of any age learn. He argues that curriculum ought to be arranged flexibly to suit individual interests and needs. Yes, all the undergraduates agreed, that would be ideal.

"But why, then," I queried, "are you teaching poetry? Or wouldn't you, if things were different?"

"No, no," one girl said, "I think we'd teach it anyway."

"Why?" I insisted.

But no one would speak. "Why are you afraid to say that you care about it?" There was a good deal of embarrassed laughter, followed by some effort to be articulate. Yes, the students agreed, they did care about it. They read it for pleasure, and they tried to write poems for pleasure. More than that, when pressed further, they admitted that they liked what most young poets were saying. Poets said what they felt and they wrote about things that mattered, in language and forms that were inventive. I suppose one could not ask for a better rationale for curriculum or a more useful way to enliven a language classroom. "Speech" after all, as Creeley puts it, "Speech is a mouth."

(Following the talks by Miss Howe and Miss Danish, the audience raised numerous questions about the open-question technique referred to by the two speakers. To answer similar questions which may occur to others, Miss Howe has given the following explanation of the open question and its value in drawing students into discussion and discovery.—ED.)

THE WHAT AND WHY OF THE OPEN QUESTION

First, the teacher does not know *the* answer to her question, but she wants to know *an* answer, to hear a response from a student. (It fosters the idea that the teacher is interested in her students, rather than in hearing her particular answer from them.)

Second, the open question opens discussion, or leads to another question, rather than to an answer that ends discussion and forces you to begin with another, totally different line. (Hence, it fosters continuity of discussion, rather than a catechism.)

Third, the purpose of an open question is never to test students on material you want them to know, nor is it to trick them into following your own line of thought, in the Socratic manner. The purpose is, rather, to encourage them to develop their own modes of response and patterns of thought. (It fosters independent thinking rather than second-guessing or pleasing the teacher.)

Fourth, the open question should encourage students to respond emotionally or intuitively and then to reflect upon those responses thoughtfully, even analytically. Thus, the open question follows the pattern of most creative writers—from feeling to consciousness.

The open questions we have used most frequently to begin discussions are "Which poem do you want to read?" (of several on a page) followed by "Why did you choose that poem?"; "Do you like the poem?" followed by "Why?"; and "How does the poem make you feel?" followed by "Why do you feel that way?" or "What in the poem makes you feel that way?"

Usually the questions lead directly into the poem, since they ask the students to announce their responses and then to attempt to develop reasons for each response either by thinking about previous experiences or by looking at the words of the poem or both. Sometimes an open question may lead away from the poem at hand to a different but nevertheless useful discussion. Let me illustrate:

You may use the open question "Do you like this poem?"

And you may get a quick "yes" or "no" in response, which you would follow up with the most open and useful of them all—"Why?" or "Why not?" You may then hear either a pet peeve or a previously learned generalization, or possibly a whole analysis:

    —I don't like poems about snakes.
    —I don't like poems unless they rhyme.
    —I don't like it because it doesn't say anything.
    —It just describes a wheelbarrow, and poems are supposed to have a message.

More open "whys" should continue to open the discussion although there is a danger in the teacher's engaging a single student for too long in dialogue. Other students may get restless, and the student thus engaged may begin to feel picked on. It is possible to open any "why" question to the group:

    —Do all of you like poems that rhyme?
    —Why do you think people like poems that rhyme?
    —Why do you think poets choose not to use rhyme?

Had the teacher decided to pursue the student who offered an opinion about snakes, the dialogue might have sounded like this:

    —Why don't you like snakes?
    —Because I was bitten by one once. I'm afraid of them.
    —Is it a valid reason for not liking a poem or a book: to say that you don't like the subject?
    —Maybe, but I can't convince my history teacher that I don't like history.

Again the question could be asked of the whole class or group: "Do all of you sometimes like or dislike poems because of their subject? And do you think that's legitimate, that you have a right to feel that way?" You might get into questions of being fair to the author, who, after all, can't be blamed for your having been bitten by a snake.

There are, obviously, no neat lessons to be drawn from such

a discussion. But the conversation should raise the level of literary consciousness in the group. Sophisticated critics are aware that their personal prejudices, often a result of particular experiences, influence their ability to respond to a particular poem. But students are either unconscious of the process or they may feel guilty about their negative responses. A discussion might reveal that everyone in the group feels negative responses about some subject or other, whether it is snakes or cats or lemons or particular sorts of people. Students might attempt to solve the question of how one deals with such feelings when one reads a poem. Certainly the discussion might be unique and never occur again, although it might continue to serve as a reference point through other hours of discussion.

RICHARD LEWIS

RICHARD LEWIS, poet and anthologist, teaches
children at the Manhattan Country School and adults
at the New School for Social Research in New York.
Several of his anthologies are composed entirely of
the creative writing of children.

A Dialogue of Poetry

I think there is no formula for getting a child to appreciate
poetry or to write poetry. There is no one way of teaching a
child or working with a child in this area. It depends on you
as a person, your relationship to children as a group and a
child in particular. I cannot impose my relationship to children
on you. You have to discover what your relationship with a
child is and then work from there.

.   .   .

Poetry is not a medicine. It isn't something to be prescribed
for children because it is beautiful or right or moral.

.   .   .

We often begin to tell children what should be read and
how it should be read and why it should be read. In most
cases, when I have done that, I have had twenty children
turned off. Not until I began to see the possibility of letting
the children come to poetry themselves, move toward it at
their own pace with their own willingness, did poetry really
begin to make sense to them. So, when I talk about "a dia-
logue of poetry," I am talking about children bringing poetry
to themselves.

.   .   .

We need to go back to early childhood, to that point where poetry seems to come out of the very rhythm of a child moving. My two-year-old daughter has created her own little poem —a very simple one. It has just one word—"eye." When she sees a dog or a bird—anything with an eye—she will stop and say, "Eye," and move her hand to her eye. The motion of her hand is connected to her word. I think it is the marvel of young children that their words are connected to the rhythms of their bodies, to the way they move, the way they dance. Some of the most extraordinary expressions of childhood do not come from a child sitting quietly in a chair, but from a child who is playing and dancing. Little children have to move. It's their way of learning, and their language is associated with that way of learning.

.　　.　　.

Questions can be very simple and yet have a profound way of reaching right down to the core of what we feel. Ask a child "What does it feel like?" or "How did you feel?" and you're asking perhaps the most important question one can ask in elementary education.

.　　.　　.

As a teacher, each of us has to become less of a teacher and more of a human being and friend to children. Somehow we have to become interrelated to their world instead of telling them what their world should be. We have to allow each child to learn that he can discover, on his own, a great many of the truths, whatever they may be, that we supposedly think we are giving to him. And that can only be done when a child begins to gain confidence in what *he* thinks and feels.

.　　.　　.

When I meet with children—whether they're six-year-olds or fifteen-year-olds—I don't take a book with me or bring a poem to read. Instead, I rely on what they're going to say to me and then try to react to what they say. I try as much as possible to key into what it is they're thinking and ride with them, rather than lure them into riding with me.

. . . .

Poetry is a means of projecting an individual voice. And the only way that individual voice is going to be heard is for the reader or listener to begin to hear his own individual voice. Often when talking to children, I ask, "Do you talk to yourself?" There's always a little murmur of giggles, and then they admit, "Yes, we all talk to ourselves." When we really get down to the truth of the matter, we find that everybody talks to himself. What is this thing we call talking to ourselves? It is listening to what we're saying to ourselves, hearing the words, the feelings, the things that are in us.

. . .

Surely in every classroom there must be certain rules and certain courtesies that have to be respected when we are working together. Often one of these courtesies is not total silence. But it is listening to what other people say and not being frightened or saying what you want to say.

. . .

The imagination is constantly at work as a sort of clearing house for information, feelings and ideas. Consequently, we must not say to a child, "We are going to have this period of time when you work creatively and imaginatively." Instead we must show children that the imagination, the artistic impulse, the desire to create is always going on. It never stops.

And it doesn't happen just in creative writing. It can happen with mathematics or chemistry or wrestling or whatever you want to give it to. It's always going on and always working. The artistic imagination is like the mathematical imagination and the historical imagination. There is an interrelation between all these things.

. . .

What we've done so much of the time is to divide the world into subjects and allot time to study these various subjects. One of the subjects we study is poetry. And the child probably has no conception that poetry is related to anything else. He doesn't see the relation between poetry and history, poetry and mathematics, and poetry and chemistry or whatever. He's lost the point of what poetry really is.

. . .

Poetry is a way of speaking about the interrelation of things.

. . .

One of the things that I do with my group of children is to give each one an empty notebook in which he can put anything and everything he wants. If he wants to scribble in it, that's his business. If he wants to write poems or stories in it, draw pictures, or not do anything in it, he can. Everything happens when you give a child that choice. In a sense each book becomes a reflection of each child. Each uses it as his own private mirror. I am constantly buying more books for the children, not because they're tearing the pages out, but because they are using them and finding ways of making language work for them. Often we call this "creative expression." It shouldn't be called that—it is just language speaking for that individual. When a child feels that language is something he owns and possesses, something he uses in a particular way, he is coming close to accepting poetry as a natural way of thinking.

. . .

In a classroom I visited once, there was a printing press which was, in a sense, a symbol to the children. Through that printing press went their thoughts. Not to be destroyed but to be recreated in the printed world for all to see. The process of writing their thoughts down on a piece of paper, putting it through that printing press and then handing it to other children was a communicative device. The children began to listen and to talk with each other, something which is very tragically absent from most classrooms.

. . .

In every classroom I have visited where there was talking going on among the children, there was often a tremendous amount of rich and personal expression coming from the children. There was no set time for writing; the writing was going on continually.

. . .

I think all children have sensitivity as a base. I think all children have feeling as a base. All children have as a base the ability, when the opportunity is presented to them, to create from that sensitivity an expression of their own feelings.

. . .

When we can get children to respond to language, to write it the way they want to and write about the things they want to write about in the form and manner they prefer, then they will have the impetus for discovering what *other* people have written.

. . .

Often a book of poetry has sat on my desk at school for weeks without being opened. The most profound teaching experience I have is when a child says, "Can I take the book home?" Profound because, in a sense, I had nothing to do with the teaching. The teaching has begun to happen within the child. He is the one who wants to learn the way he wants to learn it. I might ask him which poems he likes. The important thing is that it's his opinion, not mine. He has begun to delve into the material himself. In essence, I'm saying: Let the materials be available. Indicate to the child that the materials are there. Let him realize that he has the talent to feel and to sense and to know. Then let him reach out. We're not saying to the child, "This is what poetry is; this is what you must learn." We're saying to him, "This is what you are, and there are other people who are involved with this same desire to understand who they are and what they feel." The impetus must first come from the child. He is the motivating factor.

. . .

I believe that all of us have within us the power of poetry, because we are what we are. And that is the very stuff of poetry itself.

EVE MERRIAM

EVE MERRIAM, the author of 30 published books
ranging from nonfiction and biography to poetry,
juveniles and humor, teaches creative writing at the
City College of New York. She and her husband,
Leonard Lewin, also a writer, live in New York with
their two teenage sons.

"I," Says the Poem[1]

"I," says the poem arrogantly,
"I am a cloud,
I am a tree.

I am a city,
I am the sea,
I am a golden
Mystery."

How can it be?

A poem is written
by some someone,
someone like you,
or someone like me

who blows his nose,
who breaks shoelaces,
who hates and loves,
who loses gloves,
who eats, who weeps,
who laughs, who sleeps,

an ordinary he or she
extraordinary as you or me

whose thoughts stretch high
as clouds in the sky,

whose memories
root deep as trees,

whose feelings choke
like city smoke,

whose fears and joys in waves redound
like the ocean's tidal sound,

who daily solves a mystery:
each hour is new, what will it be?

whose life unfolds its own golden key

"I," says the poem matter-of-factly,
"I am a cloud,
I am a tree.

I am a city,
I am the sea,

I am a golden
Mystery."
But, adds the poem silently,
I cannot speak until you come.
Reader, come, come with me.[2]

It's the "I" of the poem that I would like to use as a spring-board.

More than any other form of literature, poetry uses "I" in the ego sense; that is, the me-myself-and-I meaning of the word: to break through the barriers that novels and plays and short stories and any other form of writing create. No characters, no middle man: instead, poetry has the ability to plunge directly into the core of emotion. It's as though you are able to rip through the entire Sunday *New York Times* and get to exactly the one line that you want.

The second sense of the "I" of poetry is, of course, the visual eye. It stands for all the senses—touch, taste, smell, sound, as well as sight. More than any other form of literature, a poem has the ability to be highly selective, to choose the significant detail, to make choices and to make comparisons in life by its uses of language.

So we have the "I" in the ego sense and the visual eye—seeing, touching, tasting, smelling, hearing.

A third "I," in a punning sense if you will, is the a-y-e I which says "Aye" to life. There again the poem has affirmative power more than any other form of literature. By the strength of its emotions, by doing away with any other character except the self, by plunging to the core of emotions, and by being so selective of the details of language, poetry plunges to depths as well as heights. Not all poems are affirmatively cheerful or hopeful; it would be a very saccharine world if they were. Yet we find that in moments of great stress we turn to poetry and our emotions become purged. Out of the most terrible despair, a poem like Gerard Manley Hopkins' "Nay, pitch past grief worse there is none," goes to the very depths of our soul and enables us to emerge on this side of life.

I thought of this power of poetry last year after the assassination of Martin Luther King, Jr. People were so moved they didn't know how to express themselves. The actual poems would have to come much later. But people marched in many places; they simply walked on the streets repeating his name in a tremendous rhythmic feeling: *Martin Luther King, Martin Luther King.* And the poem became the spaces between the syllables.

This triple power of poetry of the three "I's"—the egotistical or egocentric "I," the eye of the senses, and the affirmative "Aye"—this is what I think gives poetry its enduring place.

Northrop Frye, in *The Educated Imagination,* says that ideally our literary education should begin not with prose but with such things as "This little pig went to market"—with verse rhythm reinforced by physical assault. The infant who gets bounced is beginning to develop the response for poetry in the place where it ought to start. For verse is related closely to the child's own speech, which is full of chanting and singing as well as primitive verse forms.

If we listen to children talking, we do not hear prose, we hear a heavily accented speech rhythm with a great deal of chanting in it or whining, depending on the mood of the child. If we are lost in a strange town and ask someone for directions, we don't get prose, we get pure Gertrude Stein. Or the teenager issuing mating calls over the telephone is not speaking prose although the speech rhythm is as formalized as prayer, which it somewhat resembles.

I bring you some research absolutely fresh from the field to bear this out. Here is a four-year-old boy on the telephone to a friend. (Nothing has been added or restored; it is not like packaged white bread in the store.)

> What's thinking?
> Nothing.
> That's strange

I'm fine
It's getting better.
See you tomorrow
How's your trains doing?
It isn't. It isn't.
We do so. We do so.
We do not. We do not.
Because I don't like it.
Tomorrow
What're you going to do then?
What? What? What?
Watermelon!
Sing it. What?
Watermelon. Watermelon. Watermelon.
Muckmelon, whitemelon, boshmelon
Boobechiemelon
Helamelon
Rogermelon
Falling down melon
London Bridge melon
Davey Crockett melon
Oakie melon
Doggie melon
Watermelon
Water diggy melon
Ogo, Gogo melon
Shoemelon
Slow down melon
Watermelon
Trainmelon
Ding-a-ling trainmelon
What did you get for Christmas melon?

That's a four-year-old. Now here is a seventeen-year-old on the telephone:

> Well, I'm practicing my guitar.
> Well, well, I don't know. All right
> Okay, okay. What?
> What? Well, that's logical.
> Who? When did this happen?
> When? When?
> Well, like the scars are kind of healed,
> I guess.
> Well, well, I don't know.
> Well, okay, okay, okay.
> I gotta go study, gotta get to my guitar.

This same guitarist on the telephone, in writing an application for college and having to give an autobiographical background, put these words down on paper:

> A rush, a rush of colors, lights
> A feeling of soundy mornings
> Waking out of silence to the day's mouths.
> Swallowed in, feel and feel warm
> Flesh, rattled bed shadows on walls sleeping.
> Swaddled in baby clothes I roared off to bed.
> Puffy winterwalks with small camel hair coat
> And large pony rides.
> Summer, the smell of the wave
> After wave after wave after wave
> On the beach
> Salt pushed up into my nostrils
> Nostrils—
> A word I always liked.

Now, the moral of that is not to let your children talk in-definitely on the telephone, but to see that sometimes these repetitive speech patterns can come off in more poetic ways. I'm a great believer in not giving up on people's powers to articulate until at least a few days after we've stopped being able to talk at all. This relationship of children to poetry is something that I think we tend to take rather skeptically, those of us who have been involved in classes.

It's all very well for somebody to say enthusiastically, "Oh, well, yes, it's there." But how do you really reach it in the children? There's no magic button to press, of course, but I think you can come to realize that children are not intimidated by poetry as we have been, perhaps because we had the wrong kind of teachers. They haven't got the wrong kind of teachers; they've got you. As Dr. Spock reassured all parents in the opening of his book, "Remember, you know more than you think you know." If you can take heart in the fact that you are a walking poem and a child is a walking poem whose heart beats with all kinds of rhythm when he is swinging along, then poetry may not seem quite so formidable.

Children, when they start to talk, do come out with remark-able things. These are not necessarily formal poems; but be-cause children's egos are so close to themselves, because they haven't had a lot of social feelings put on top—they haven't learned how to be gracious, how to delay—they respond im-mediately. They have to make comparisons out of the only world they know. So they begin using similes and metaphors long before they know what they are. I wouldn't care if the teacher never used the word "simile," never used the word "metaphor," just let the images come. Never mind what they are called formally.

Here's one from a four-year-old, trying to figure out what a wrench is:

A wrench is a relative of a pliers.
Like cousins, or like kangaroos
To other jumping animals.
Like the tin Woodman and the Scarecrow
Only they're relative friends.

Children come out with what seem to us to be surrealist ideas, but they aren't really. These youngsters are trying to make sense out of the world. A three-year-old asks, "What color is Chicago?" It's not a bad question, is it?

A five-year-old chants,

I want someone to sleep with me.
When I wake up early it's dark
And desperate
And I feel dangerous
It makes me nervous.

Has none of us felt that way? I have, often.

Now the same child crooning to his mother:

When you're cranky
Go take a nap
I'll cover you with a flower.
When you wake up, you'll be all uncrossed
And I'll give you applesauce
And you can sprinkle the cinnamon on yourself.

I would like to use the three forms of the "I" of a poem and consolidate them: the ego "I," the seeing "Eye," and the affirmative "Aye." In the two following poems, the bride and groom are portrayed at the moment of exchanging their vows. We're told that at the moment of drowning, one's whole life flashes before one's eyes. I haven't yet had that experience, but I have had the experience of marrying, and it seemed to me that much of life does seem to get into that very brief moment between the time of that split second when you say the "I" and the "do."

THE BRIDE

"Aiaiai
Eye
I
    from the sky of ocean
    from the arch of father mother
    from the warm wet cave
    from the cradle the curb the comb
    from safe from standback from straightedge
    from the ledge of window street school
    from the black slate wiping clean with chalky
    white
    from friends from flower beds
    all neat-edged skirt-hemmed bush-hedged
    to a stranger
    to the wild curve of the polar unknown
    feathery
    freezing
    flying
Do."

THE GROOM

"Ay
Eye
I
    from the aerodrome of ocean
    from the well of mother father

from the cave the spring the deepest greenest flight
from flinging up on the sandy shore
from heavenly mother hailing gust of father
from how will you make your living on drydark land
my babymanboy
from don't play with dreams those are wet dirty don't
touch
from the hand shoving up from the hand slapping
down
from father speaking his silence
from mother counting her empty purse
from games and shouting and books and banners and
cheers
from strangers' chairs

> to the home I've never known
> that I lived in all along alone
> to warm with lights and softest curtainings
> to flowers in a bowl
> the scarlet petals unfurling unfading
> the green water fresh forever

Do."[4]

The second part of " 'I,' Says the Poem" that I would like
to discuss a bit is that I am a tree "whose memories root deep
as trees." Poetry has the power of language to go back, to have
memories, to restore us in a time when we desperately need
the restorative values of language. Our language has become
debased by the mass media. We know this and we sit around
and we groan about it. In governmentese you get the delib-
erate obscuring of language. In advertising one of my favorite
debasements is the phrase "frozen fresh," and you get a glass
of orange juice. Another one which I like very much—"cigars
factory fresh." I came across one when I was taking the bus

here yesterday: a sign: "To be erected soon on this property an industrial park." In the supermarket you find that Ideal is a dog food, Life is a cereal and a cigarette, Joy is a detergent. We have to go to poetry to restore us after this cheapening debasement. Why does poetry do this more than other forms of literature?

Partly because of its direct way of not using characters but using feelings and of being so freighted that each word counts. You can't just throw words away in a poem without thinking about what they mean and without having to give them a special weight.

We're lucky, I think, that we have the English language to work with, because it is so rich in ambiguity. I don't mean ambiguity in the murky sense that one writes and it's not possible to tell what the meaning is, although, of course, there are different layers to get, but the fact that so many words in English have the ability to offer different interpretations as does the word "I" that we were talking about before.

I came across a fascinating book with a rather repulsive title, *The Mind Builder*. It sounds as though you have to get up in the morning and, in addition to your physical exercises, practice ten minutes of building up your mind. But it really is an interesting book by an Englishman named Richard W. Samson. In his comments about ambiguity in language, he noted the words that have a single meaning each. I was fascinated to find what rather *recherché* words they were. So many words have more than one meaning that Mr. Samson was quite hard put to find words that had only a single recorded meaning each. One of the examples he gave was "hemialgia." (If you've ever had a neuralgic pain on one side or part of the body, you have no ambiguity about it. There's only one meaning to this word.) However, words like "man," "tree," "watch," "fan" and "circle" have more than ten meanings apiece. You can get more than two hundred meanings for the word "set." "In," of course, you can use as an adjective, adverb, noun, verb or prefix. Nineteen sixty-eight was the great "in" year. We had be-ins and sit-ins and love-ins. My favorite was at Bryant Park in New York City, behind the public library, where one of the stores put on a fashion show and called it "A Mink-In."

One of the most ambiguous words I can think of is "it." This is a poem about the word "it" called

BASIC FOR IRRESPONSIBILITY

IT is a useful word.
IT can do many things.

IT cannot shine,
the sun does that.
But IT can rain,
and IT can snow.

IT can look like trouble ahead.
IT can look like the end of nonviolence.
IT can even look like another war.
I would not want IT to happen,
and you would not want IT to happen,
but we have nothing to do with IT.

IT is not my fault
anymore than IT is your fault
IT is nobody's fault.
IT is just the way things are.
That is the way IT goes.

IT goes by itself.
We do not have to approve of IT.

We do not have to do anything about IT.
That is the best way for IT to grow.[5]

Another rather ambiguous little word is "they." I have written
a poem about "they" called

BASIC FOR FURTHER IRRESPONSIBILITY

THEY is another useful word.
You can use THEY to scare people like on Halloween.
BOO!
THEY say there's going to be a long hot summer
starting early and lasting all year round.
BOO!
THEY say more people just don't understand law and order.
THEY say some people have to have law and order
forced on them.
That's what THEY say.
I don't and you don't
but that's what THEY say.
It's easy to play THEY.
You don't need paper or pencil or a ball or a net or a stand
　or any kind of base for support.
THEY just make it all up and we go along.[6]

I think that if we can keep in mind that poetry is one of
the best ways to remove ourselves from the debasement of
language and come back to illuminating the root powers of
words, this will help us to combat the intellectual smog not
only in our own world but even in the children's world. The
children are assaulted by these same things that we are today.
This, of course, is one of the very many qualitative differences
between this age and generations before. The mere fact of the
existence of television (to say nothing of the other mass

media) has transformed everything so that the children are getting debased language before they are learning their ABC's. They are learning to be grammatically incorrect before they know whether it's correct or not. "Winstons taste good, like a cigarette should." Every child knows the couplet.

The power of poetry has to become more potent and much more necessary. Poetry cannot in this day and age be considered something extracurricular or something that one can use in a secondary way as enrichment. It's basic. You've got to have it or the language will perish.

The third point that I would like to make about the " 'I,' Says the Poem" is what the poem says at the end: "I cannot speak until you come." This is the oral necessity for poetry. In this day and age our kids are oriented not to reading but to hearing, to vocalizing. Perhaps they can be turned to poetry.

I would have two rules for poetry that I would enforce absolutely in what I hope would be a benevolent autocracy. First, I would insist that every poem be read aloud. Second, I would insist that it be read twice, even if a person dislikes it or finds it impossible to comprehend. In poetry you are dealing with twins, identical twins—words and music coming together in the same space. As the medium is in the message, so the poetry is in the music and the music is in the poetry. You simply can't have one without the other. This again is one of the delights of language, and I urge you not to turn up your nose at things like word games or puzzles or jumping rope or any kind of physical exercise or mental agility. All of these things lead to the behind-the-scenes power of poetry to work with alliteration, repetition, onomatopoeia—all of the forms that we know the names for but we really don't need to. Never mind drilling with the names. Just working the effects out in language is much more important.

Today we have the standard joke that goes on all the time:

everybody talking, talking, talking, and complaining, "I can't communicate. I can't reach you. I can't dig you. You don't know what I'm really saying. We can't communicate with each other. Rap, rap, rap." We're suffering from this terrible, terrible prosaic overcommunication, the overkill of verbiage. What a relief to be able to come to the briefer, more concentrated form of poetry, which is really saying something instead of all this communionless palaver. Here is an example of the kind of communication that I mean.

COMMUNICATION

Communication is a wonderful thing.
It is a wonderful thing
when two people can really
communicate together
and date together
and mate together
and go on to create together
a communicating family.
See?

The family that communicates together
is a wonderful thing to be.
The greatest, United Statest family to be.
Mommy has a telephone in her kitchen.
She communicates with Daddy
who has a telephone in his hobby basement.
Sister has a telephone in her canopy bedroom,
Brother has a telephone in his den.
And the baby, the sweet little family baby,
has a plastic rattle and a real telephone in its crib.

Hello, hello, are you there?
Everyday we can call each other up and say

Hello, hello who are you, who am I?
Hello Mommy Hello Daddy Hello sister, brother bay-bee
dolly baby hello hello hello.

You can dial your mother direct you know.
What father are you calling please?
I'm sorry, but that sister is not in working order.
Brother has been temporarily disconnected.
And the baby, the sweet little family baby,
has a telephone cord attached to its navel
and around its neck.

Hooray, hooray for the communicating family.
We go on picnics and beautifying highways together.
We do not litter or loiter to look at the scenery.
We drink our family-size Coca Cola
and save the bottles to bring back
and throw
used-up father and mother
away.
Goodbye!
Hello!
By By!

As another example of how our children are affected by
this culture, which doesn't seem to have a place for poetry
in it, and why we need to become pioneers anew and restore
language to them, here's a very brief portrait of today's city
child:

CITY CHILD, CITY CHILD

I know that oranges grow on a tree,
I see the frozen-juice commercials on TV.

I know where the milk comes from that I sip,
I saw a cow in a comic strip.

City children are deprived and so are city parents, and so also are country children and country parents, because we are all in a city culture nowadays. Not only in this country but worldwide. I think this is the way it's going, and the best spray we can have against that verbal fallout is to use poetry in the best way we can. An ancient Egyptian is supposed to have said, "Poetry is vocal painting, as painting is silent poetry."

The vocal is the important part, I think. I remember once sitting with a group of kids when Archibald MacLeish was on television reading his poems, and one of the youngsters said, "Well, of course, when you read it out loud, it understands itself better." That seems to me to make very good sense. When you read it out loud, it does understand itself better.

One of the experiments which I think is always possible, of course, is to use children together to create group writing. You don't even call it anything as formal as a poem if you don't want to. Sometimes it works; sometimes it doesn't.

One of the charming examples of that came out of a working-class school in Paris. Four- and five-year-olds were asked to give their explanation of what the origin of the world was. They came out with a joint composition on the origins of man. You will notice that the first "I" we spoke of—the ego—is close to the child's concept:

THE ORIGINS OF MAN

No papas no mammas no waitresses!
Not even Father Christmas, but then
where were all the people?

Perhaps in the wind, or in the clouds, or in the sky.
Me I was on the sun! Me on the stars!
Me in the moon!
We really don't know where, but surely within our Mamma.
In that time there were only beasts, plants, cereal and onions!
And then, the earth came forth, the sea went to other places
and it left the countryside.
And it's like in Paris now there's no more ocean.
Then in Paris when the sea went away
When it stayed only in the sand
There came men to fight the giants
There were no Davey Crocketts or Buffalo Bills or Zorros.
There were men who wrestled with gorillas
Who were very strong and hit with stone
Who didn't know there was iron in the earth
Or metal in the earth.
They didn't know how to make use of such things
that are in the earth.
They didn't know there was a treasure in the earth.
We, we know!
Now, everybody knows.

That reminded me of the words of an American child of a similar age who also used the visual eye to select details, not thinking that he was making up a poem particularly. This was a concept:

> I'm simply wonderful.
> I know all about everything.
> I know all about the world.
> How to put on a belt.

It is kind of wonderful to learn how to put on a belt, isn't it? It may be that someday somebody will do a graduate

thesis on the belt, the girdle of the world, and the circum-
ference and the cuddling and embracing feeling we all want.

Another quote that I would like to share with you is what
Carlyle said about Tennyson. He said, "Alfred's always
carrying a bit of chaos around with him and turning it into
cosmos." That really is poetry's job and poetry's joy. It can
range from the very miniscule level of the little boy encom-
passing the world by learning how to put on a belt all the
way to the profundity of Gerard Manley Hopkins or Blake or
Shakespeare.

I think what is most important is to bear in mind that live
poetry is ourselves, the way we breathe, our bodies. Poetry
is all the things that go on everyday.

The last thing in the world that poetry is is poetic. When
artificial additives of fancy language are put in, poetry be-
comes like flavorless foods loaded with gum arabic and sodium
benzoate and all those things which preserve it so there is no
more resemblance to the real thing than a can of deodorant
labeled "Lilac" resembles a real lilac bush blooming in the
spring. A lilac bush in the spring resembles Whitman's
superb poem about Lincoln. It has nothing to do with this
other world of lilac detergents. Please avoid poetics in poetry.
Avoid the kind of thing where one has fairies creating things
rather than nature. Nature is better than any fairy that any-
body ever made up.

Let me read what I would call an anti-poem. It's no poem
at all because it encompasses things like this coy singsong:

SNOW

The snow's a snuggly blanket
The fairies tuck around
The sleeping posies in their beds
Safe in the crumbly ground.
They cover all so gently,

And softly say, good-night,
Then steal away and leave them
All snug and warm and white.

Never mind the fairies. Show the kids a book of photographs of snow crystals. Ostensibly the same shape, each one is totally different in design. What could be more miraculous or more wonderful for a child to appreciate than snow as part of nature, as part of the world he inhabits? He doesn't need Walt Disney figures with cheesecloth and little gold halos on their heads coming down to make the snow, because the snowflakes have this individuality. Similarly each person has great individuality with a different voice, a different thumbprint. Yet all of us share the same human race: unique and the same. This is the power of poetry in a prosaic world.

NOTES

What the Heart Knows Today

1. MOIRA DUNN, "Writing Poetry in the Elementary School," *Elementary English*, March, 1968.
2. NANCY LARRICK, "Life Ain't Been No Crystal Stair," *School Library Journal*, March, 1969.
3. From *Breakout*, published through Operation Adventure of the International Institute of Los Angeles, August 30, 1968.
4. *Ibid.*
5. RANDALL JARRELL, *The Bat Poet* (New York: The Macmillan Co., 1963).
6. PATRICK GROFF, "Where Are We Going With Poetry for Children?" *The Horn Book*, August, 1966.
7. JAMES STEPHENS, *The Crock of Gold* (New York: The Macmillan Co., 1912).
8. MYRA COHN LIVINGSTON, ed. *A Tune Beyond Us* (New York: Harcourt Brace Jovanovich, Inc., 1960).
9. JONI MITCHELL, "Michael From Mountains" (New York: Siquomb Publishing Corp., 1968).
10. SIMON AND GARFUNKEL, "Bookends" (New York: Charing Cross Music, Inc., 1966).
11. SIMON AND GARFUNKEL, "Richard Cory" (New York: Charing Cross Music, Inc., 1966).
12. THE BEATLES, "Getting Better." Lyrics reprinted from *The Beatles Illustrated Lyrics,* edited by Alan Aldridge (New York: A Seymour Lawrence Book, Delacorte Press, 1969).

13. SIMON AND GARFUNKEL, "At The Zoo" (New York: Charing Cross Music, Inc., 1967).

14. PABLO NERUDA, *Bestiary/Bestiaro* (New York: Harcourt Brace Jovanovich, Inc., 1965).

15. HAROLD TAYLOR, "The Arts in America," *Colorado Quarterly*, Fall, 1965.

The Poetic Language of Childhood

1. JOHN HALL WHEELOCK, *What Is Poetry?* (New York: Charles Scribner's Sons, 1963), p. 69.

2. From *Writings from Outdoor School*, by Grades Five and Six. Teachers: Patricia Heringer, Peter Hinds, Gerald Scovil, Janet Wither (Milwaukie, Oregon: Seth Lewelling School, May, 1966).

3. RALPH J. MILLS JR., ed. *On the Poet and His Craft* (Seattle and London: University of Washington Press, 1965), p. 145.

4. WHEELOCK, *op. cit.*, p. 27.

5. The children's writings in this paper have come from New York and Oregon. The author is indebted to both parents and schools. The following schools are represented: St. Ann's School, Brooklyn; Bank Street School for Children; City and Country School; P.S. 134 and P.S. 108, Manhattan; and Seth Lewelling School, Milwaukie, Oregon.

"Talk to Mice and Fireplugs . . ."

1. Copyright © 1971 by Karla Kuskin.

2. KARLA KUSKIN, *The Rose on My Cake* (New York: Harper & Row, Copyright © 1964 by Karla Kuskin).

3. KARLA KUSTIN, *In the Middle of the Trees* (New York: Harper & Row, Copyright © 1958 by Karla Kuskin).

4. KARLA KUSKIN, *Alexander Soames: His Poems* (New York: Harper & Row, Copyright © 1962 by Karla Kuskin).

5. KARLA KUSKIN, *Roar and More* (New York: Harper & Row, Copyright © 1959 by Karla Kuskin).

6. KARLA KUSKIN, *Square As a House* (New York: Harper & Row, Copyright © 1960 by Karla Kuskin).

7. KARLA KUSKIN, *Alexander Soames: His Poems, op. cit.*

8. KARLA KUSKIN, *In the Flaky Frosty Morning* (New York: Harper & Row, Copyright © 1969 by Karla Kuskin).

9. KARLA KUSKIN, *Alexander Soames: His Poems, op. cit.*

It's Not a Joyous City

1. GWENDOLYN BROOKS, *Selected Poems* (New York: Harper & Row, 1959).
2. ARNA BONTEMPS, ed. *Golden Slippers: An Anthology of Negro Poetry* (New York: Harper & Row).
3. Reprinted by permission of his agent, Mrs. Isabel K. Heller.
4. EVELYN TOOLEY HUNT, "Taught Me Purple," *Negro Digest* (February, 1964).

Experiment in the Inner City

1. ROBERT CREELEY, *Words* (New York: Charles Scribner's Sons, 1964).
2. GREGORY CORSO, *Gasoline* (San Francisco: City Lights Books, 1958).
3. WILLIAM CARLOS WILLIAMS, *The Collected Earlier Poems* (New York: New Directions Publishing Corp., 1938).
4. *Ibid.*
5. WILLIAM JAY SMITH, *Poems 1947–1957* (Boston: Little, Brown and Co., 1957).
6. WILLIAM CARLOS WILLIAMS, *op. cit.*
7. KENNETH PATCHEN, *Collected Poems* (New York: New Directions Publishing Corp. 1939).

"I," Says the Poem

1. Copyright © 1969 by Eve Merriam.
2. EVE MERRIAM, *It Doesn't Always Have to Rhyme* (New York: Atheneum Publishers, Copyright © 1964 by Eve Merriam).
3. EVE MERRIAM, *The Double Bed from the Feminine Side* (Cameron Publishers, Copyright © 1958 by Eve Merriam).
4. *Ibid.*
5. Copyright © 1969 by Eve Merriam.
6. Copyright © 1969 by Eve Merriam.

INDEX

Academy of American Poets, The, 59, 70
Adams, Henry, 25
"Addition Problem" (Goode), 66
Adults, poetic need of, 57
Advertising, Language of, 156
Affirmation, poetic role of, 149–66
Alcindor, Lou, 83
Alexander Soames: His Poems (Kuskin), 41, 44, 48
"Alice's Restaurant" (Guthrie), 3, 4
Allegorical writing, 60–61
American Folk Songs for Children (Seeger), 50
Anglund, Joan Walsh, 51
"April 4, 1968" (Goode), 64
Art, poetry and, 41–42, 44
"At the Zoo" (Simon and Garfunkel), 20

Baez, Joan, 16
Baltimore City Public Schools, 112
  experiment in, 112–40
"Basic For Further Irresponsibility" (Merriam), 159
"Basic For Irresponsibility" (Merriam), 158–59
Bat-Poet, The (Jarrell), 11
Beatles, The, 4, 26
  influence of, 16, 18–19
  rhythm of, 33
  songs of, 17–18

Beaver College, 101
"Bestiary" (Neruda), 21–23
Bethlehem Steel Company, 51–52
"Birds Flying South" 36
Black children and teenagers, *See* Inner-city Youth
Black consciousness
  poetry about, 78–79, 83–84, 93–98
  white reactions to, 98–105
Blake, William, 165
Bought Me a Cat and Other Animal Folk Songs (Seeger), 50
Braun, Henry, 107, 120–21
"Bride, The" (Merriam), 155
Brooks, Gwendolyn, 73
Brown, Sterling, 89
Bryant, Juanita, 68
"Bugs" (Kuskin), 41
Bush, Terri, 62

Carlyle, Thomas, 165
Carroll, Lewis, 44
Caswell, Leroy, 124
Ceballos, Olga, 9–10
Chaucer, Geoffrey, 18
Children and youth
  city, 162–66
  black and Puerto Rican
    attitude toward city, 74–77
    workshop of, 62–72
  ego, affirmation, and senses of, 147–66
  encouragement of, 49–50
  inner-city

Children and youth
  inner-city (*Cont.*)
    black consciousness of, 83–
      84, 93–105
    poetry of, 8–10
    reactions to poetry, 73–77
    workshop of, 62–72
  motivation of, 146
  poetic language of, 27, 28
  preschool, playful poetry of,
    30–31
  reactions of, 46–47
  reality, discovery of, 35–37
  relationship to poetry of, 56–
    59, 140–46
  rhythm of, 32–35
    response to, 44
    speech, 150–56
  sensory images of, 28–30, 142
  attitude toward teachers, 8
Church of the Open Door, 62
  workshop at, 62–72
Classroom procedures, 13–14, 20–
    26, 49–55
  colors and, 51
  singing, 50
  See also Teaching ideas
Ciardi, John, 53
"City Child, City Child" (Mer-
    riam), 162–63
Cohen, Leonard, 16
Coleridge, Samuel, 18
Collins, Judy, 3, 16
Coltrane, John, 89
"Communication" (Merriam),
    161–62
"Complete Destruction" (Wil-
    liams), 122
"Congo, The" (Lindsay), 44
Contemporary thought, poetry as
    expression of, 131
Corso, Gregory, 2, 75, 107
  poetry of, 116–17

Crawford, Deborah, 67–68
Cream, The, 16
Creative writing
  browsing as a lead to, 70
  encouragement for, 141–46
  experiment in, 108–40
  facets of "I" and, 147–66
  freedom of expression and, 81,
    89–105
  growth and, 27–29
  Haiku and, 45, 53
  honesty in, 12
  identity motivation of, 78–80,
    166
  inspiration and, 87–93
  invention and, 131–33
  learning conditions for, 86–96
  motivation and, 136–37
  new forms for, 10–11
  open-question discussion and,
    118–40
  playfulness and, 30–32
  protest, 10, 17–18, 25
  publication of, 63–72
  reading and, 39–48
  teachers and, 11–12, 24–25
  workshop for, 62–72
  See also Language; Poetry
Creativity Research Institute, 2
Creeley, Robert, 108–9, 137
Crock of Gold, The (Stephens),
    14
Cummings, e. e., 107
  discussion on, 120, 123–24
Curriculum, organization of, 137

Danish, Barbara, 106–40
"Darkling Afternoon" (Holmes),
    68
Dawson, Juan, 78–105
  poetry of, 93–98
"Day in the Life, A" (Beatles), 18
"Death" (Dawson), 93

Dickinson, Emily, 45
"Dew" (Minor), 66–67
Discussion, open-question, 108–40
    purpose of, 137–40
Disney, Walt, 166
"Dog Around the Block"
    (White), 75
Doors, The, 16
Doty, Warren, 78–105
Drawing, reading aloud and, 41–
    42, 44
Drugs
    heightened consciousness and,
    19
    poetry on, 132–33
Dylan, Bob, 33

"Eagle, The" (Tennyson), 120
Economic pressure, expression of,
    8–10
Educated Imagination, The
    (Frye), 150
Ego, poetic role of, 147–66
Elementary English, 7
Eliot, T. S., 39
Emotions
    creativity and, 147–66
    encouraging expression of, 140–
    46
    in poetry, 11
Environment, 88–105
Establishment, protests against,
    17–18
Every Time I Climb a Tree (Mc-
    Cord), 54
Experimental teaching, 108–40
Expression, freedom of, 81, 89–
    105

Facenda, John, 95
Ferlinghetti, Lawrence, 2, 75
Fiorenza, Michael, 124
Fisher, Aileen, 50

Folk songs, 2–4, 50
Freedom of expression
    creating environment of, 89–
    105
    refusal of, 81
Freedom Schools, Georgia
    (1965), 75
Frye, Northrop, 150

deGasztold, Carmen Bernos, 54–
    55
"Getting Better" (Beatles), 17
Ghetto, poetry of, 5, 8–10
Gilbert, W. S., 44
Gill, Michael, 69
Goode, Michael, poetry of, 64–66
Goucher College, 106
    teaching experiment and, 108,
    112–13
Grammar, children's, 63
"Grasshopper" (McCord), 34
Green Is Like a Meadow of Grass
    (Larrick), 52–53
Groff, Patrick, 11–12
"Groom, The" (Merriam), 155–
    56
Gross, Ronald, 120
Guthrie, Arlo, 3

Haiku, 45, 53
"Halloween," 31
"Harlem" (Hughes), 75
"Harper Valley P.T.A., The," 4
Hate poems, 8–10
Heath, James, 78–105
Henderson, David, 107
Hendrix, Jimi, 16
"Highwayman, The," 45
Holmes, Anthony, 68
Holt, John, 136
Hopkins, Gerard Manley, 149,
    165
How Children Fail (Holt), 136

Howe, Florence, 106–40
Hubbell, Patricia, 75
Hughes, Langston, 75–77
Hunt, Evelyn Tooley, 77

"I've Seen Enough" (Meyer), 67
I Like Weather (Fisher), 50
Identity, motivation and poetry, 78–80, 166
Inner City Mother Goose, The (Merriam), 5
Inner-city youth, 78–105
  attitude toward city, 74, 77
  black consciousness of, 83–84, 93–105
  criticism of teachers by, 80–93
  freedom of expression and, 81, 89–105
  identity motivation of, 78–80
  language of, 99–100
  learning conditions for, 86–93
  poetry of, 5, 8–10, 78–79, 83–85
  reactions to poetry of, 73–77
  white authorities and, 79–82
  workshop of, 62–72
Inner-city schools
  experiment for, 108–40
  problems of, 106–8
Inspiration, inner-city teenagers', 87–93
"Integration Poem, An" (Dawson), 95–97
Invention, poetry and, 131–33
"Invictus," 15
Iolanthe (Gilbert), 44
"Is God Dead?" (Radcliffe), 76–77

"Jabberwocky" (Carroll), 44
Jarrell, Randall, 10–11
Jiménez, Juan Ramón, 18
Johnson, Reginald, 114

Johnson, Richard D., 133
  poetry of, 132–33
Jones, LeRoi, 2, 102–3, 107
  popularity of, 2, 101–3
Jordan, June, 56–72
Joyce, James, 44
Jump-rope jingles, 4

Keats, John, 6
Keller, Helen, 117
Kennedy, Robert, 40
King, Martin Luther, Jr., assassination of, 40, 64–65, 149–50
Kuskin, Karla, 38–48

Language
  ambiguities of, 157
  children's poetic, 27–37
  communication and, 161–62
  creativity and, 141–46
  debasement of, 156–160
  discovering reality through, 35–37
  freedom of, 81
  interpretation of, 74–75
  memory power of, 156–60
  popular music, 16
  use of, 130–31
"Language, The" (Creeley), 108–9
Larrick, Nancy, 1–5, 8, 49–55, 73–77
"Last Night I Drove a Car" (Corso), 116–20
Lauter, Paul, 116n
Learning
  conditions for, 86
  motivation and, 136–37
  teachers experiment in, 108–40
Leaves of Grass (Whitman), 21
Lehigh University Poetry Workshop, 49

Lennon, John, 16
Lewis, Claudia, 27–37
Lewis, Richard, 141–46
"Light" (West), 84
Lincoln, Abraham, 165
Lincoln University, 82
Linda X, poetry of, 71–82
Lindsay, Vachel, 44
Livingston, Myra Cohn, 6–26
Lloyd, Wesley, 114
Lorca, Fedrico García, 18
"Lucy in the Sky with Diamonds" (Beatles), 18

McCord, David, 34, 54
McKuen, Rod, 16
McLuhan, Marshall, 3
Malcolm X, 94
Merganthaler Vocational-Technical High School
    poems by students of, 124–27, 132–33
    teaching experiment in, 113–40
Merriam, Eve, 5, 75, 146–66
"Michael from Mountains" (Mitchell), 17–18
Midsummer Night's Dream, A (Shakespeare), 39
Mind Builder, The (Samson), 157
Minor, Carlton, 66
Minstrels, 3
Miss Ebonette Beauty Contest, 105
Mississippi Freedom School (1964), 106–7, 116n
Mitchell, Joni, 4
    music of, 16–17
Monkees, The, 33
"Mood, A" (Wardaw), 85
Mother Goose rhymes, 50
"Mother to Son" (Hughes), 75
Motivation, learning and, 136–37

"Mummie Slept Late and Daddy Cooked Breakfast" (Ciardi), 54
Music
    drugs and, 19
    as experience, 3
    invention in, 16–18
    poetical role of, 2–3, 50
    pop music and lyrics, 16–20
    protest, 17–18
    symbolism of, 17, 19
"My Life" (Bryant), 68

Naturalness, poetry and, 79–80, 92
Negro Digest, 77
Neruda, Pablo, 7
    poetry of, 21–23
"Nice Day for a Lynching" (Patchen), 134
    discussion of, 135–36

O'Conner, Mike, 124
Ohio Wesleyan, summer program at, 91–92
"Old friends, old friends/Sit on their parkbench like bookends" (Simon and Garfunkel), 17
Old Possum's Book of Practical Cats (Eliot), 39
Onheiser, Ronnie, 124
Open-question discussion
    experiment in, 118–40
    purpose of, 137–40
Oral-language culture, 3
"Origins of Man, The" (Merriam), 163–64

Parents, protests against, 18
Patchen, Kenneth, 2
    poetry of, 134
"Pied Piper of Hamlin, The," 45

Playfulness, lead to poetry, 30–32
Poems of Earth and Space
  (Lewis), 27
"Poet" (Smith), 130
Poetic language, 27–37, 130
Poetry
  children's choices, 4–5
  construction of, 44–45
  contemporary thought and feel-
    ing, 131
  discovering reality through,
    35–37
  drawing and, 41–42, 44
  experiencing, 3
  hate, 8
  human purpose of, 56–59
  language of, 130
  meaning of, 45, 47
  misuse of, 6–8
  music and, 3–4
  nature of, 133
  participation in, 3–4
  playful, 30–32
  poetic form, contemporary,
    131
  publication of, 63–72
  reading aloud of, 39–48, 160,
    163
  reality and, 4–5
  recorded for listening, 2
  remembering, 60
  rhythm, 32–35
  role of ego, senses, and affirma-
    tion in, 147–66
  sensory image, 28–30
  sound construction of, 44
  upsurge of, 1–5
  values in use of, 130–37
  writing of, 163
Poetry Search, 1–2
Poetry Search Anthology, The, 2
"Pop Poem" (Gross), 120
Pop music, *see* Music

Prayers from the Ark (de Gaszt-
  old), 1, 54–55
Preschool children, playful poetry
  of, 30–31
Protest poems, 10, 25
  songs as, 17–18
Publication, children's poetry, 63–
  72
Puerto Rican children
  attitude toward city of, 74–77
  workshop of, 62–72
Pushkin, Aleksander, 18, 103

Race relations, attitudes toward,
  89–105, 133–36
Radcliffe, Martin, 76–77
Radio, effects of, 3–4
"Rain," 52–53
Rawls, Lou, 95
Reading aloud, 39–48
  choice of poems, 40–42
  drawing and, 41–42, 44
  experiment in, 108–12
  material choice for, 40–42
Recordings, importance of, 2–3
Relationship multiplication, po-
  etry and, 61–63
Reznikoff, Charles, 75
Rhodes, E. Washington, 95
Rhythm, children's speech, 32–35,
  150–56
"Richard Cory," 17
Roar and More (Kuskin), 41–43
"Roaring Wind, The" (Minor),
  67
Robinson, Samuel, 78–105
Roethke, Theodore, 7
  on rhythm, 32

Samson, Richard W., 157
Sanchez, Michael, poetry of, 9
Sandburg, Carl, 75
Seeger, Pete, 50

Senses, poetic role of, 149–66
Sensory images, 28–30
Sentz, Doug, 124
Shakespeare, William, 18, 165
    adverse effects of, 16, 18, 80,
        95, 101–4
"She'll Be Comin' Round the
    Mountain," 50
Shelley, P. B., 35
Simon and Garfunkel, 4, 16, 23
    music of, 17, 20
Simon Gratz High School, 78
    black studies at, 89
Singing, classroom, 50
Smith, William Jay, 130
"Snow," 164–66
Social pressure, expression of,
    8–10
Speech rhythm, children's, 150–
    56
Splain, Lonnie, 124
Spock, Dr. Benjamin, 153
"Spring and All" (Williams), 130
Square as a House (Kuskin), 43
Stein, Gertrude, 150
Stephens, James, 14
Swenson, May, 75
Symbolism in popular music, 17,
    19

Tale of Two Cities (Dickens), 91
"Talk to Mice and Fireplugs," 38
"Talking" (Goode), 65
"Taught Me Purple" (Hunt), 77
Taylor, Harold, 26
Teachers
    as arbiters, 7
    choice of poetry by, 15–26
    goals for, 137–40
    inner-city
        children's attitude toward, 8
        criticism of, 107–8, 117–19
        experiment for, 108–40

teenage criticism of, 80–93,
    104
poetry misuse of, 6–8, 15
Teachers and Writers Collabora-
    tive, 112
Teaching experiments, inner-city,
    108–40
    evaluation of, 127–31
    open-question procedure, 137–
        40
    student-centered, 108
    students' reaction to, 114
    teachers' reaction to, 115–16
    undergraduate, 111, 127
    writing of, 122–27
Teaching ideas
    children's rhythm and, 150–56
    communication of, 159–62
    creativity and, 141–46
    drawing as, 41–42, 44
    expression in, 26
    facets of "I" and, 149–66
    inner-city teenagers and, 80–
        105
    language power, 156–60
    reading aloud, 39–48
    relationship multiplication, 61–
        63
    sound construction, 44
    workshops for, 62–72
Teenagers, inner-city, see Inner-
    city youth
Television, influence of, 3
Tennyson, Alfred, 120, 165
"This is Just to Say" (Williams),
    131–32
"This Man" (Jordan), 59–60
Thompson, Glen, 68–69
Three Dog Night, 16
Time, 46
"To Algebra" (Lloyd), 25–26
"Towards an Impure Poetry"
    (Neruda), 7

"Trees," 34–35
Tune Beyond Us, A (Livingston), 16
"Turn, Turn, Turn," 3

Undergraduate teaching of poetry, 111–27
Underprivileged youth, *see* Inner-city youth
"Unite" (Dawson), 97–98
Upward Bound program, Yale Summer High School, 1

"Village Blacksmith, The," 1, 15
Voice of the Children, The, 63–72

"War," 37
Wardlaw, Romani, 78–105
  poetry of, 84–85
We Real Cool (Brooks), 57
West, Veronica, 78–105
  poetry of, 83–84
What Color Is Love? (Anglund), 51
Wheelock, John Hall, 28
  poetry definition by, 35
"When I Went Out to See the Sun" (Kuskin), 41
"When You're Lying Awake" (Gilbert), 44
Which Horse Is William? (Kuskin), 43
White, E. B., 75
White authorities, attitudes toward
  children's, 9–10
  teenagers', 79–105
Whitman, Walt, 21, 23, 165
"Who Am I" (West), 83–84
Wilkinson, Jean, 73
Williams, William Carlos, 2, 107
  poetry of, 122, 130, 131–32

"Witches Ride, The" (Kuskin), 40–41
Words, root powers of, 159–60
Wordsworth, William, 133
Workshops, inner-city, 62–72
"Wrestlers, The" (Braun), 121
Writing, creative
  encouragement of, 141–46
  experiment in, 108–40
  facets of "I" and, 147–66
  freedom of expression and, 81, 89–105
  growth and, 27–29
  Haiku and, 45, 53
  honesty in, 12
  identity motivation of, 78–80, 166
  inspiration and, 87–93
  invention and, 131–33
  learning conditions for, 86–96
  motivation and, 136–37
  new forms for, 10–11
  open-question discussion and, 118–40
  playfulness and, 30–32
  protest, 10, 17–18, 25
  publication of, 63–72
  reading and, 39–48
  teachers and, 11–12
  workshop for, 62–72

X, Linda, poetry of, 71–72
X, Malcolm, 94

Yale Alumni Magazine, 1
Yale Summer High School Upward Bound Program, 1
Yeats, William Butler, 18
"Yes . . . We Learned" (Sanchez), 9
You Read to Me, I'll Read to You (Ciardi), 54
Youth, *see* Children and youth